Jane Wolfe:
The Cefalu Diaries
1920 - 1923

with Commentary by Aleister Crowley

Compiled and Introduced by David Shoemaker

Jane Wolfe (circa 1919)

Jane Wolfe:
The Cefalu Diaries
1920 - 1923

with Commentary by Aleister Crowley

Compiled and Introduced by David Shoemaker

Published by

The Temple of the Silver Star
P.O. Box 215483
Sacramento, CA 95821

www.totss.org

First Edition, August 2008

First reprinting, February 2017

ISBN-13: 978-0-9976686-3-6
ISBN-10: 0-9976686-3-6

Published by

The Temple of the Silver Star

A Not-for-Profit Religious Corporation
David Shoemaker, Founder and Chancellor
(Donations, legacies and bequests made to the Temple of the Silver Star
are tax deductible in the United States.)

The Temple of the Silver Star
Founded in Service to the A∴A∴

INTRODUCTION

by Dr. David Shoemaker

Do what thou wilt shall be the whole of the Law.

"June 30, in Bou-Saada, alone." As she wrote these words--the first words you will read in these diaries--Hollywood actress Jane Wolfe patiently awaited her destiny. She had travelled from the United States to begin her studies with Aleister Crowley at the Abbey of Thelema in Cefalu, Sicily. Crowley was to become her lifelong teacher and friend; indeed, she was one of the few friends Crowley retained from the Cefalu period to the very end of his life. Wolfe's studies at the Abbey with Crowley, from 1920 to 1923, would serve as her foundational training for the remaining decades of her life, and she became one of Crowley's most important aides and confidantes as Thelema (and specifically, Ordo Templi Orientis) spread to the United States.

Wolfe played a vital role in the dissemination of Crowley's thought and magical practice in several important ways. As a pivotal participant in the O.T.O. community in Southern California from the late 1930s through the mid-1950s, Wolfe was able to convey much of the essence of Crowley's system of training to the local initiates, most of whom would never have the chance to work with Crowley in person. Furthermore, her student in the A∴A∴, Phyllis Seckler (who later took the magical name Soror Meral), went on to teach Crowley's system to multiple generations of students into the twenty-first century. Seckler also played a crucial role in the resurgence of the O.T.O. in the 1970s, birthing much of modern Thelemic culture as we now know it, and bringing the seminal work of Crowley and Wolfe full circle.

The diaries collected here represent the bulk of surviving material from Wolfe's Cefalu period, lovingly preserved by Soror Meral for many decades, and presently residing in the archives of the Temple of the Silver Star. Sadly, many months of diaries were lost in the years after Wolfe left Sicily. However, she later attempted to reconstruct some of the lost periods, and we have included those summaries here. Many of these diary entries were originally handwritten, and later typed for evaluation by Crowley. Crowley's handwritten comments are laced throughout these pages, giving valuable insights into his teaching methods and state of mind during this pivotal period of Thelema's development. The diaries also give a vivid sense of daily life at the Abbey, and the nature of the relationships among its primary residents.

Wolfe's work at Cefalu was that of a beginner. She did many months of preparatory work, including basic practices in asana, pranayama, and assorted meditation techniques. This work culminated in her admission as a Probationer of A∴A∴ under Crowley on June 11, 1921, a few days before she began a thirty-one day magical retirement in a tent on the beach near the Abbey. Unfortunately, no diaries exist for this retirement, but as with other such gaps we have included summaries written by Wolfe at a later date.

Much of the present material is quite legible and well-organized. There are, however, segments of handwritten diaries which are oddly dated, creating some confusion as to their proper chronological placement. I have attempted to organize such entries into the most likely and logical order possible. Additionally, some handwritten segments (including a few of Crowley's comments) are faintly written, or otherwise difficult to decipher. I have adjusted the exposure and contrast of these images to make the material as clear as possible.

As you can likely imagine, holding and examining these diaries in person immediately transports the reader back in time to the Abbey. The intensity with which Wolfe pursued her Great Work, lovingly typing her entries for Crowley's review, is palpable as the pages are turned. It is for this reason that we have chosen to present these diaries in facsimile format for this publication. We hope that what is sometimes lost in legibility is recovered in the pleasure of seeing these entries just as Wolfe and Crowley left them over eighty years ago. Most of all, it is our hope that readers of these diaries will be inspired to continue and intensify their own Great Work, including the all-important practice of the magical diary, for this is truly the best way to honor the life and work of those whose hands created these pages.

Love is the law, love under will.

Sacramento, California
August, 2008 e.v.

June 30. In Bou-Saada, alone. Wondered, concernedly whether I had failed in any particular. Napped in afternoon, entirely. Slept so sound I was not conscious of going to sleep or of waking, but received "Ordained of God". This gave me comfort.

Night of June 30. In confused dream A. said: Had I not failed in some particular stance, we could be together sooner. This very confused & I think not true vision.

July 1 – I take it that I am here to acquire silence – become a part of the Great Silence. And this I must achieve alone? Why the silence of Aleister?

I notice that when lying down I breathe more regularly than in California – this without thought.

Last night I flew much, centre of necessary effort in chest region. Freud?

July 7. Here since June 25, and while not depressed have been calm over alone ness. Last evening Bébé seemed to hurry away from the French lesson, as though weary of me. For the first my spirits flagged and sank. And the leeches got busy! For twenty-four hours I struggled against their hold. Then this evening at seven was there poured into me a blessed stream of love. It filled my being and overflowed and left me with renewed strength, peace and understanding. It is Creative Love I must encompass here. That my lesson of Bou-Saada.

     Dignity, patience, confidence,

July 9 – Dreamed last night that as a woman of an older race, having certain mental freedom I compiled a small geography - a small, square book, with various coloring on the cover. Is not geography more modern?

July 11 - The spinal bulb or the cerebellum, which? It must be the former if I reason correctly. Here is where Love lodges & from whence comes dignity of spirit. When force flows to or from here, there is force of mental as well as permeating love.

July 27 - Cefalù - A blank - I get nothing.

28
11.50 - 12.05 pranayama 20.10
6. - 6.15 pranayama & asana 20.10

10.30 Read part of ————— so certain ————— described
     in ————— of Solomon the King.

July 29 - morning finished copying occult record
10.28 - 10.40 pranayama 20.10

          Reading "Het Dangerous".

30 - asana 5 - 7
          "   3.40 desire to swallow - overcome by focussing on it
                 3.25
                    26 muscle of neck near spine twitched once
                 3.27 3 fingers of right hand   "   "
                 3.37 Swallowed
                 3.40

Afternoon bathing.

How is this? The mind of A.C. so gigantic, his experiences so vast & of such an intense nature that, not having a proper resting place, a sea in which to bathe that shall satisfy all needs during the periods of rest, he has to resort to what seems almost violent reactions? i.e. The jructures to ordinary mortals are violent in expression of outline + color + "distortion". Here is Capable of a performed suddenness.

31 —   praṇāyāma from house to top of elevation at beach
Asana , 10, 25 — from returning — 10 min.

10.35 Thumb of left hand moved

43 middle finger of same.

10.45

10.45 } Dharana, Outlined triangle, flame colored
5.1 } could not Held 1 almost continuously, but
had constantly to recall other 2 lines — at times
totally unable to do so — again triangle disappeared
+ I could not bring it back. Felt this might be
due to fatigue due to previous "Neauli" exercise,
do discontinued;

10,53 – 11,13 Hatyogeeshes. No steadiness + at no time natural.
3rd entire body — only head + shoulders.

Aug 1 – 6.02 – 6.22 Asana
6.12 – back of left hand irritated
6.14 – throat automatically contracted — one swallow.
At intervals right knee moved very slightly.

6.22 – 6.42 Dharana
could not obtain disk steadily at any time — no
No time yellow, she light, toward left side. Last 5
minutes no disk at all but held position, At times
before this no disk though something assured
me there was a disc — this assurance gone last 5 min.

6.42 – 6.53 Hatyogeeshes
could not reach this properly at all at any time.

(Tired)

Slept half an hour
wakened ... towards morning by raps on shelf
111 (guess) – 11 (correct) In Cal. my guides were most careful not to
distract me when tired. what waked me here when sleep
even needed?

First vision for A.C. Olive orchard

During my 3-day guest period, Crowley tested tested me on Astral Vision.
This way: He threw "the Sticks" of the Yi King. The symbol that turned
up was imaginatively placed on a door; one opened the door, walked through,
and followed az he felt urged. I walked along the little traveled way of an
olive orchard unril I saw before me a tall figure in a striped robe, with a
tall striped headpiece - Egyptian I think. He looked me over, and I passed
on to a one-story flat-roofed building, to face a long altar, with nothing
on it. But above was a large silver moon somewhat like the golden sun one
in occult works. There came to the altar a man, black-haired and wearing
a red abbai, stiched in gold. He turned and looked at me. Instantly I
shut off the vision, for it was Crowley.

There were a few other tests, or trips, but I do not now recall them.
Many of my diaries were destroyed when the Abbey goods werd shipped to
London. As we are on the matter, let me say Crowley syarted me on Astral
Visions. He had magnificent sigils for such use. There form of use:- You
place the sigil at a suitable place for yourself, look at the sigil for a
few minutes, drop your eyes to the floor (my methid, for I kept my eyes open,
or close them. Then give yourself to your work and travel through Astral
regions. That is: if you are ready for it. Making your own sigils is excellent, if you know what forces to depict on your sigil.

As a result of my inability to tell A.C. of my vision on arrival at Palermo there remained a barrier. And because of it Ninette Shumway and I were thrown together, A.C. felt the strain, and another house was taken. The 'Horsel' -- Abbey for Leah and A.C. The "Umbilicus" for the second house because the children were housed there. Also the food was there prepared by Ninette. I worked on my practises and typed the MMS. Meantime trying to sleep outdoors on o on our mattresses, and make friends with the creeping insects of the night.

In the Abbey was "The Circle" as we named it, where the Rituals were performed morning and evening.

The Temple room was brilliantly painted by A.C. His work taught me to appreciate. His work taught me to appreciate the brilliant colours of the palette. The paintings on the wall were Crowley's work. Mine was the colouring of the symbolic designs on the floor. A round altar in the centre. At the East a small one on which were placed the figures of one-time gods of the past., Dionysus, for example. In front of this sat A.C. Again, in front of him, a splendid altar for incense dedicated to Pan. The robes of the group were blue: hoods lined with red.

The Cauchenaur. Here I left somewhat of my work on the walls. These walls were named : Heaven; Earth; Hell.

True these walls were covered with what could be called obscene. But one learns to accept things, just as a child does until its mind is poisoned by his elders, whether grown-ups or boys. In London one day I saw a child of four snickering and sniveling of a painting of the nude. A child of 4! When a student wished to work in the Temple; others, including A.C. - absebt-ws himself.

Cefalu.

There were dear little fellows of 4 to 6 at this time. And how they didi
adore being with their mothers. But this did not satisfy A.C. The boys had
to break the Gordion knot. So, sandwiches were packed, the boys were ordered
to take a walk somewhere, anywhere. Hansi behind trees did not last long.
Our little boys took themselves hither and non, exploring the countryside
Hansi frequently returning with a trailing robe, or none at all. Howie was
always clothed. But Hansi was a little animal of the woods. The peasants
adored him and gav him their superb bread I would be glad if such breed
bread like that came my way to-day. Hansi had manna frm heaven at all times.
As Leah was busy with Crowley's work, I taught the boys poetry, the stars
and planets.

It was a ddelight to see Hansi going to the bottom, picking up she lls put
½ut there for his enjoyment. Howir could not relax.   O, yes, he stayed on
on the water but in a stiff struggling manner.

On my first trip to the beach I took with me - and put on - a black woolen
bathing suit I bought in Cefalu. The only one who covered herself. It reminded me of a one-time studio girl who had gone to Russia. After a few swim
clother, she became ashamed by her isolation - as all the others were nude --
and she finally took off her germent and became one of the many, and so nejoy-
ed the water without shame.

It was astonishing how the Italian children screamed and hid their faces h
mot hrt'd skirt. Italian boys, by the way, clothed themselves in mother's
undies when tumbling around in the water. They could not swim in what they
had on. All this prepared me for my 31 days alone on the beach when on Retirement in the tent of Aleister Crowley.

There was a part o the Beach separated by a projection of rock. Few people went there, possibly because the descent to the beach was steep, possibly smaller than the other beach, and more rocky. Here is where A.C. decided

Cwfalu

I should take a Magical Retirement. He consulted the Hexagram, cast "The Sticks", turned up the result, put, 6 meditations. Rge first week one-half hour for each meditation; second week 1 hour for each subject; 3rd week one-and one-half house for each; fourth week 2 hours each subject. But Liber Thisarb, at the end of the Ritual, had to be shortened. I had heard of levitation as a result of Pranayama (breathing according to time periods. On my last day at t e Beach, my body held steady its posture, but slowly slowly tipped over until it lay easily on the canvas of the tent without breaking asana

Cefalu

(1920)

First Equinox in Cefalu, when A.C. and Leah were in Naples, Ninette with her

dry humour, broke the ice and made me laugh - preciou s laughter. Thereafter

I was relaxed, and slowly adjusted myself to my surroundings, Fleas and mas-

quitos No, I did not; Fleas were of 3 sizes: large, medium, and small - the

hardest to catch. I got use to the biteing, but not the creeping- up and down

the back - and elsewhere. Ninette was a hot bed for them. Bugs - for a short

season; thank heaven.

Meabtime I had taken up my studies with A.C.

(1920) Twice)   A. Asana; control of posture - completely still
        a   )   B? Regularization of breathing; Pranayama.
)   C Dharana; Control of Thought
        Day)   D Avtral Travel, using Shaddai sigil which belongs to Yesod
)   on the Tree of Life at this juncture.
Work was written out fully to receive A's comment.

We played "Fives" on our court; went swimming in the Mediterreab; Rock Vlimb-

ing, small or large. Long walks up the hills of Sicily; and such activities

out doors. Painting on the inside, walls in brilliant colours as one chose.

The Abbey Temple in the Magical colours necessary to the Temple. I did thé

floor work; A.C. telling me the olours, designs, etc. We enjoyed the work,

and became a united group.

1920

July 31

Pranayama from house to top of elevation at beach
    4 inhale, 4 exhale. 1/2 hr.
    Return, 10 mins only.
Asana - 10.25- 10.45 p m thumb & finger of left
                            hand moved.
Dharana 10:45-10:50 Too fatigued to continue long-
                er ʉ - 'Vision' work responsible?
~~CRITERNXXXE~~
10:53-11:13 Harpocrites. No steadiness and at no
                time visualized entire body - head &
                shoulders - no color.

Aug 1

6:02-6:22 Asana 6:12 back of left hand twitched
                6:14 throat automatically contract-
                    ed - no swallow.
                Right maxxi knee moved little.
Dharana 6:22-6:42 No time color, last five mins:
                no square at all nor could I
                imgine one.
Harpocrites 6:42-6:53 Could not reach this prop-
                erly at any time. Tired

Asana 11-11:15 Accomplished nothing, confusion in
                    house left me quite unnerved
        Attempted Dharana, but without success.
        In very bad condition.
Pranayama 2:40-3:05 to bath. 4-8 to top of hill
        4-4-8-4 from hill to beach.

Asana p m 10:30-50 Broke once.
Dharana 10:50-11:10 Little better work then here-
                tofore, but sleepy at times.
                (Due to hot milk I think)
11:12-32 Harpocrites

Aug 2

6:30-6:50 Asana
    -- Four times right arm contracted
        6:45 Throat automatically contracted.
6:50-7:10 Dharana
        Swallowed twice; other bodily movement
7:12-33 Harpocrites. Very poor.
        Started Temple of Solomon The King.
9:50-10:05 Pranayama 4-4-8-4
10:05-10:10   "   4-8-8-4
10:10-10:20   "   4-4-8-4
        Rest
10:50-11:10 Asana   Eye shifted in all about half inch
            Desire to swallow came & went but 11:07 yielded
11:10-11:30 Dharana Emotional tried to enter; con-
                quered this; some bodily movement.
11:35-11:55 Harpocrites Better silence than hereto-
                fore, changed thumb at lip.

Pranayama to beach, 4-4-8-4 Broke once top of sec-
    ond elevation - cont'd
10:10-10:30 p m Asana Left ankle aching. Throat
    suddenly dried and cough.
10:30-10;50 Dharana
10:55-11:12 Harpocrites. Last few minutes body re-
    acting to mosquitos & flea. Controlled reasonably
    for a time, then body twitched violently as
    from electricity.

Vision work.
    Ocelli, taken as word on which to work.
        Got exterior of temple, grey stone, door-
    way outlined as I have seen pictured on Egyp-
    tian temples; priest in front in long robe, color
    of this robe suggested rich cream of old lace;
    right hand raised though could not locate it, but
    it came between me and priest - high head-dress
    on priest, thought I saw stripes, it was dark
    and I think had some blue.
        Interior - great height, large pillars, 3
    in number on either side, 3 on left side in more
    light than those on right. Beyond pillars 3 steps
    running width of temple, a level stretch, then
    3 steps, level floor of 6 or 8 feet to altar.
        In centre silver globe from which
    radiated many luminous spokes.
    Priest in front of altar, in crim-
    son robe with gold decoration
    around shoulders, back to me. He
    turned and as he did so I noticed
    silver globe was directly over his
    head, making a continuous line with
    his body.
        No words spoken.

Aug 3 6-6:20 Asana Throat contracted 2 - other slight
    disturbances but cannot recall.
    6:20-6:40 Dharana Principal intrusion of thought
        lines from 'Adoration'. Also found myself say-
        ing 'Yellow square' when losing it.
    6:45-7:05 Harpocrites
    On hill. Heretofore I have been in a school house
        where were placed before my vision beautiful
        pictures, understanding love and resulting sym-
        pathy. Art - arare, to plow - life a fine
        achievement, outer and inner. Was given the
        principles and theoretical work. Now I am placed
        outside and confront facts, some of which amaze
        me. Speculation regarding these cause of rest-
        lessness at night? Will watch this.
    '777'
    10:45-11:05 Asana. Coughed once.
    11:05-25 Dharana Improvement here.
    11:30-50 Harpocrites Finished badly,

Pranayama to beach and half way back 4-4-8-4
10:05-25 Asana Held body fairly well
10:25-40 Dharana Made a mistake, broke this too
           soon - ankle & leg not quite so pain-
           ful
10:45-11:05 Harpocrites Elbow extended - different
           result from elbow dropped to side.

a/

Aug 4 Disturbing influence all night. Tried to say
          Pentagram, but only certain words, could
          not utter all but cannot remember which
          words these were.
6:15-35 Asana. Swallowed at 6:30
6:35-55 Dharana Very poor indeed.
7:00-20 Harpocrites Never got into this in any
          way but held position.
9:33-53 Pranayama 4-4-8-4 On intake and hold
          tried making myself one with strength
          of earth & sea.
          '777'
          Pranayama 15 mins

a/

10:45-11:05 Asana Eye shifted 3 times
11:05-25   Dharana A rigidity from morning.
          11:20 relaxation, worked better.
11:30-50   Harpocrites.
          Pranayama to beach & ½ way back, 4-4-8-4
10:10-30 Asana Broke once

a/

10:30-40, 45 Dharana Hopeless. Coughed, body
          twitched, mosquitos & flea
10:50-11:10 Harpocrites First half unsuccessful
          Held second in a measure.

Aug 5 Thought I had solved sleeplessness. Evidently not.
          Still wakeful and '777' running around like a
          mantra. Later, one came, put right hand on back
          of my head, left forward and over left temple &
          forehead (I was lying on my right side) and gave
          me an iron key, rather short handle, lock-opening
          part about 1½ inches. In handle-end was welded
          ring, hanging loose as link of chain.

Step all such
things with H.P.K.

6:05-25 Asana. Asana Coughed - as this broke
          posture, killed mosquito.
6:25-6:40 Dharana. Made a mistake, broke too
          soon. Accomplished something, but poor
          sitting.

a/

6:45-55 Harpocrites After ten minutes stopped &
          worked for equilibrium. Condition where
          I could fight on slightest provocation.
7:57-8:05 Pranayama 4-4-8-4
8:05-15   "   4-8-8-4
9:10   Tao Teh King I need music.
          This helped a lot. Feel better. Have
          been far away from Love.

Aug 5 10:30-50 Asana Frequently by the time finished
with Dharana have forgotten physical
manifestations in Asana.

10:50-11:10 Dharana. Better. Locust sang continuously by me without disturbing poise
nevertheless stillness not so good. Elbow in pain, right hand numb. Wrong position.

a/ 11:15-35 Harpocrites.

10:25-45 Asana
10:45-11:23 Dharana
Do not understand lack of comment -
probably asleep.

a/ 11:05-23 Could not get Harpocrites at all. Held
position and maintained silence with-
out visualization.

Aug 6 6:05-25 Asana. Moved left arm off knee once -
swallowed twice.

6:25-45 Dharana. Got result in beginning only -
held position and looked where square
should have been.

a/ 6:47-7:05 Harpocrites. Could not visualize.
Tremendously sleepy. Slept instantly
after responding to tom-tom; waked
with effort 3 mins. after and felt
heaviness throughtout which I could
not master.

No pranayama.
Body utterly weary, due in greater or
lesser degree to menstrual period - though
not entirely as I think being waked mornings from sound sleep shocks system.

10:30-50 Asana.
10:50-11:10 Dharana. Started in one posture, held
5 mins & assumed posture used in present
Asana. Some results tho cannot get color.
Swallowed 2.

a/ 11:13-34 Harpocrites. After 12 mins. moved. In
some respects best so far - got babe entire and strong silence.

11:55 After above exercises lay down for complete
relaxation 11:45. Objective finally still:
found myself by solid, high grey stone
wall, large gate through which I could not
see, rounded top, Gothic style though not
pointed and placed iron key in lock. This
interested me so much, became active and
lost all.

Should have been. However, not willed.

19:15-35 Dharana. Beginning poor and ended by

observing spot where square should have been
10:35-55 Asana. Good physical. Mental good in
         spots.
10:59-11:20 Harpocrites. Could not get this. Held
            position, mental still. At 11:15 suddenly
            felt nausea.
            At writing still conscious of stomach.

Aug 7 6:10-30 Asana.
       6:30-50 Dharana. Not good, physical poor.
       6:53-7:15 Harpocrites. Physical good, vision
                 poor, also silence.
                 On hill. Feeling good physically.
       8:05-20 Pranayama. 4-8-8-4
               Tried 4-12-8-4 but either cannot do
               this arrangement or should attempt from
               the start
       8:30-9:45 '777' All this time making diagram &
                 working in alphabet. After such achieve-
                 ment need pranayama.
                 Pranayama, vigorously, 4-8-8-4. Discard-
                 ed 'earth & sea' strength, realized my
                 own.
       10:15 Tao. 'There is no house of death in his
                  whole body'.
       10:32-52 Asana. Good physical for 15 mins. Then
                fly persistently dwelt in my nostrils,
                making minute investigations. Held for
                a time, body began twitching, chills ran
                over me & I blew it off.
       10:52-11:12 Dharana. Started poorly. Right knee
                   swayed slightly at intervals, swallowed
                   2, resisting 3 other similar desires.
                   Toward finish got steadiness of mind -
                   no color.
       11:15-35 Harpocrites. Steadiness of mind, but not
                a success. The pesky locust bothered me.
                Shall look for another Bo tree.

Handwritten annotations in left margin:

a/

a/

Good: Keep on till
you can ignore such.

a/
No: Here's only
One Tree.

Handwritten annotations at bottom:

Please put in A.M. & P.M. or use 24 hour system.

Explain conditions more fully, as if writing for public.

Aug 7 (Cont'd)
p m   Pranayama to beach. From house to tope of second
        elevation 4-8-8-4; from there to beach 4-12-8-8.
9:50-10:20 Asana Thunderbolt. Leg swayed once, right arm
        moved slightly 3, diaphragm spasmodically expand-
        ed & contracted - strong desire to cough all thro.
10:10-30 Dharana, yellow square. Excellent opportunity to
        note difference between this & preceding concentra-
        tion. At no time was I conscious of throat.
        (Throat has been tickling as if from slight cold)
10:35-55 Harpocrates. Physical good, vision not. Had to
        fight sleep continuously. For first time got
        alien color: drops of red, little lighter in color
        than blood, floated downward. Got this stopped.

Aug 8.
A M
6:10-30 DHARANA, yellow square.
        Did something here, tho little. Fighting sleep,
        mosquitos biting which distracted. But I have
        discovered if mosquito unmolested, after first
        few moments of pain, any desire to scratch grad-
        ually passes away. ~~Desexmosquito~~
6:30-50 ASANA, Thunderbolt.
        Physical fair, flies walking over body causing
        chills. Mental poor.
6:55-7:15 HARPOCRATES.
        Poor.
9:00-10 PRANAYAMA. 4-8-8-8, 5 mins. Could not continue
        hold of 8 counts without breath. For remaining
        5 mins. alternated the above with 4-8-8-4, find-
        ing this required more concentration.
'777'   '777'
        PRANAYAMA, 20 mins. 4-8-8-4
10:35-55 ASANA, Thunderbolt.
10:55-11:15 DHARANA, yellow square.
        Got some results, yellow & square, part of
        time yellow flowing over lower edge of square.
        Snarled up somehow to-day as concentration af-
        fected physical sight.
        Head moved once, right arm turned half way
        round by series of small jerks. Swallowed. Lo-
        custs to-day not disturbing as yesterday.
11:25-45 HARPOCRATES.
        Not good. After repeated attempts to visual-
        ize, without success, straightened out & com-
        posed body outside & surrounding physical (What
        in the world does this mean?) This rested me,
        went back & visualized first blue shell, then
        babe. Though have done better.
P M

        PRANAYAMA to beach.
10:32-52 ASANA, Thunderbolt. Twenty minutes continuous
        fight with sleep, three times consciousness

left - eyes swam.
10:55-11:15 DHARANA, yellow square.
Still battling sleep. Four times body pitched,
several times caught body just before pitch.
Walked around room to wake up, water not cold
enough to be effective.
11:20-40 HARPOCRATES.
Walk did no lasting good. Body almost fell
over once. Again, right arm dropped.

Aug. 9.
A M
6:35-55 DHARANA, yellow square.
Did not catch one good vision of yellow square.
6:55-7-15 ASANA, Thunderbolt.
Physical fair, constant bringing back of wand-
ering mind.
7:20-40 HARPOCRATES.
Did not get into this. Entire time taken in
efforts to keep babe or blue shell before mind's
eye. Mosquito biting.
8:53-9-15 PRANAYAMA. 4-8-8-8, 5 mins
4-8-8-4,17 "
TAO, 'Forethought at the Outset'
'The Workings of the Tao'
Slept & waked, and slept again.
Must take pranayama to rouse for concentration.
10:30-40 PRANAYAMA, vigorous, 4-8-8-4, 5 mins.
4-12-8-4, 5 "
10:45-11:05 ASANA, Thunderbolt.
Positive attitude, alive. When first sitting
body & mind rather negative. Have been trying
for this positive state heretofore but without
sufficient result to note.
Eye wandered remained in radius of 1/4 inch
except for one flash of about inch distance.
Flies & ants tho not on face.
11:08-30 DHARANA, yellow square.
Not quite so positive as preceding, mind continually hopped about, pinned it down part of
time with 'This one thing I do'
11:35-55. HARPOCRATES
Have no difficulty in getting blue, why the
fight with yellow?
Picture incomplete, running around from one
to other of its parts.
For first time seem a trifle invigorated by
these exercises. Slept well last night & this
morning, mind rested. That may account for it.
P M PRANAYAMA to beach 4-8-8-4
Felt peevish while sitting on court this evening for about one hour, condition then passed
away. Do not know what caused it.

10:08-28   ASANA, Thunderbolt.
                    Another prolonged fight with sleep. Why this
change from wakefulness? I slept to-day on
the hill, again after tiffin. Felt drowsy all
evening.

10:30-50   DHARANA, yellow square.
                    Continuous fight with sleep. Beginning of
period the desire to sleep seemed to leap at
me. The vigor to continue seemed to result
from battling. At 10:45 this stopped and came
a negative, dead sleepiness, more difficult to
cope with.
Left hand pressing down on knee during this.

10:55-11:15 HARPOCRATES
                    Could not hold babe long enough to get into
blue shell. Still desire to sleep in control.

Aug 10
A M
6:15-35   ASANA, thunderbolt.
                    Notice head has a tendency to come forward &
downward, but am not conscious when movement
takes place.

6:37-57   DHARANA, yellow square.
                    Could not get this & could not bring focussing
point at usual distance place - a long way off.
Discovered I was using physical, right elbow,
neck & torse contracted. Mosquitos biting almost a relief.

7:00-20   HARPOCRATES.
                    Could not get into this at all.
On hill.
EQuinox V, Introduction to study of Qabalah.
Did not get far into this when I became sleepy.
Slept till 9:30.

9:35-10:03 PRANAYAMA
                    4-8-8-8, alternating 4-8-8-4 for 10 mins.
4-8-8-4 balance of time. Find I cannot hold
breath for 8 counts and continue more than 5
mins. Tried this method of alternating, think-
I might be able to continue longer.
At some time each day I notice a new vigor, it
does not last long but is encouraging. Result
of a combination of things. Present exercises,
physical and mental. May, 1918 I was told:
'Cease your chatter, wait for God.' This referring to a habit of continuously mouthing words
though the lips were silent. Am more diligent-
ly practising this, though when I do 'chatter'
(and this habit which I thought almost con-
quered has returned here with a particular ve-
hemence at intervals.
There is not the activity in lower back of head
heretofore referred to.

10:37-57   ASANA, thunderbolt.
        After 15 mins noticed body leaning heavily on
        right arm. At same time became conscious of
        throat. Find I can control desire to swallow
        by focussing on some definite part of body. Now
        confronted throat as a trial. Succeeded for 3
        mins. then throat hurriedly contracted, no
        swallow. Contraction suggested a relaxation
        of vigilance.

11:02-22   DHARANA, yellow square.
        Continuous conflict between attempt to vizualize
        and hearing hand drill on rocks. Found a part
        of me watching for next blow. Emotional tried
        to enter & tell me this effort was likely to
        cause injury, at the same time something within
        shrinking at each blow. Conquered this but could
        not eliminate sound of drill.

11:20-50   HARPOCRATES
        Got babe at times but unable to connect with
        blue shell.
        Find I am contracting muscles in these exercis-
        es. Must watch this.

P M   PRANAYAMA to beach.
9:37-57   ASANA, thunderbolt.
        Another fight with sleep.

10:00-20   DHARANA, yellow square.
        Physical poor, work poor, fighting sleep.
        Saw white light, about size of a dime, above
        eye line to my left.
        Later saw a light to left & about max level with
        solar plexus. Think this had a suggestion of
        violet.

10:25-45   HARPOCRATES.

Aug 11
A M
6:05-25   ASANA, thunderbolt.
        Good physical- no, fought sleep.

6:27-47.   DHARANA, yellow square.
        Saw yellow square 2, saw dark square, no square
        Left hand in pain, left leg spasm once, swall-
        owed once. Sleepy.

6:52-7:12 HARPOCRATES.
        Better than preceding but could not achieve
        any degree of stillness. Vizualised babe on
        lotus, at times blue shell. Again got alien
        color. Quick flash of J.W. in pongee colored
        silk robe with peculiar pattern of salmon pink
        around borders. Saw large wagon in country
        standing still. Lea doing something but did
        not see what.

8:10-35   EQUINOX V, Qabalah.
8:37-9:08 PRANAYAMA, 4-8-8-4

[Left margin handwritten notes:]

You can't forget a thing by thinking of it. Get interested in another thing & it's gone

Very bad

Possibly good

Took up Qabalah again` Am getting hold of
something and find it interesting.
Do not know when I put book down but must have
had ¾ hr sleep.

10:40-11:02 ASANA, thunderbolt.
Right great toe moved. This strange as I cannot consciously move this toe without moving
others. Or did another move without my noting
it?
Am I in a groove? Again came sleepiness
though nothing violent.

11:05-25 DHARANA, yellow square.
Watched any desire for sleep. Think now tense
sleepiness of Aug 9 started up wrong method,
i.e. pushing the mind. Ten minutes before I
could focus then discovered rigidity.
Entire body affected. Left leg stiff, knee &
ankle 'set', conscious of back, right buttock
paining more or less, left one numb.

11:30-45 HARPOCRATES.
(?)

11:58
P M   Just waked from a 'cat nap' - felt the need.

PRANAYAMA to beach, 4-8-8-4

9:37-57 DHARANA, yellow square.
Good method Not sleepy. Levelled mind by saying: 'Yellow
square is a part of the God-Body'. I then
could look calmly, dispassionately, imperson-
ally.

9:57-10:12 ASANA, thunderbolt.
Naturally. A miscalculation. Watched left leg. This posture cause of pain in left hip which interferes
when playing 'Foot-ball Fives'? Entire left
leg protesting.

10:20-40 HARPOCRATES.
All equally Maya - Accomplished something in the beginning - mind
& Tat! skipping about thereafter. Caught myself speculating as to whether insect on body was fly,
flea or ant.

Aug 12
A M
6:25-45 DHARANA, yellow square.
? Rather passive sitting. Principal intrusion
Ritual heard for first time last evening.
Swallowed 2.

6:45-7:05 ASANA, thunderbolt.
6:45- 7:05 HARPOCRATES.
Started out fair, ended lamely.

7:05-25 ASANA, thunderbolt.
(. Mind & body quiet at start. After 10 mins mind
quite wobbly, body indolent. Swallowed hurried-
ly, leaping in, at a moment of abstraction.

8:45-9:00 PRANAYAMA.

```
8:45-9:00      PRANAYAMA.
                    4- 8-8-4,  5 mins
                    4- 8-8-8,  5 mins
                    4-12-8-8,  5 mins
                    Gave out after third.
9:15-10:05     EQUINOX V,
                    Kabalah.
10:05-45       Sleep.
10:47-11:12    ASANA, thunderbolt.
                    Mind & eye wandered. Ant bit me. At third bite
                    gasped & knocked it off.
                    Think this decided reaction linked up with a
                    California experience, when a large red ant
                    one a m poisoned me so thoroughly by a vicious
                    bite that I had no relief until xxxxxxxxx
                    xxxx I fell asleep that night.
11:15-35       DHARANA, yellow square.
                    A lightness of body I never experienced in
                    this work - due to will to hold body relaxed?
                    Swallowed once, mind skipping about in Algeirs
                    & States. Yellow square for a time above line
                    of vision. While a part of me desired to look
                    up held to original focussing point. Noticed
                    people passing.
11:40-55       HARPOCRATES.
                    Started out well.  Three bites, at third body
                    broke down with gasp and groan - emotional re-
                    action. Started again - leaf falling from tree
                    was shock.
P M            PRANAYAMA to beach.
                    4- 8-8-4, 5 mins
                    4-12-8-8, 5 mins
                    4- 8-8-4, balance of time.
                    Enjoyed bath. Took 3 definite swims. 72, 82,
                    100 strokes. Also swam between rocks lying
                    close together where water was rough. Have
                    kept head under water 14 strokes, body coming
                    to surface on sixth stroke.
                    At dinner for a moment felt lightness of body.
                    Watched this, no other change noticeable.
9:00           Said Pentagram - Shummie and I alone.
10:51-11:12    ASANA, thunderbolt.
                    Swallowed after 12 mins. This bad, for in this
                    case mind was floating around Tunis.
11:15-35       DHARANA, yellow xquare.
                    Beginning poor. Boy outside singing, which I
                    heard continuously.  Afterward found Self
                    occupying thoughts.
                    Finished better - body light and in a warm
                    glow.
10:40-55       HARPOCRATES.
                    Stopped as forepart of head hurting.  Did the
                    method cause it, that's the question? This
                    glow of body seems definitely in outer cover-
                    ings.  Got one crocodile for first time.
```

AUG 13
A M   Wakeful during night, but this not due to
             restless mind. Rather to physical. All mus-
             cles sore & painful - from yesterday's swim?
             Head aching slightly.

6:15-35   ASANA, thunderbolt.
             Body stupid, mind started journeying. Body
             aching when finished.

6:35-53   DHARANA, yellow square.
             Something accomplished.

6:55-7:17   HARPOCRATES.
             Rested me wonderfully this morning.

8:12-30   PRANAYAMA.
             4-8-8-4. Body inclined to rigidity when start-
             ing. When walking must wear shoe that gives
             support to right instep. Relaxed arches &
             middle toe of right foot collapse without sup-
             port.
           The physical affects the mental. Here am I with
             a weakened, protesting body, head in bad condi-
             tion, and where even Laotze proves inadequate.
             What does the Hindu ascetic accomplish by in-
             flicting agonizing pains upon himself?
           'Nothing more elastic and yielding than water,
             preeminent to dissolve things rigid and re-
             sistant.'
           'God moves along the line of least resistance.'
           I cannot study, I cannot read this morning. So I
             lie quiet and still, letting flow into my con-
             sciousness whatever of Life and Beauty these
             hills, the birds, the passing winds may afford.
             Should I do aught else? At present I cannot
             think so.
             ---- In darkness, no life in me.

10:52-11:12 ASANA, thunderbolt.
             Got still here.

11:14-34   DHARANA, yellow square.
             Accomplished something, possibly because my
             first temptation to omit. Each minute seemed
             ten. Swallowed three times, once when fly was
             walking around my nose.

11:34-45   HARPOCRATES.
             Weary, weary.

P M   No Pranayama to beach, tried but could not
             continue.
             Two particular swims, which heretofore I felt
             might prove beyond my powers.

10:28-48   ASANA, thunderbolt.
             Score 1. I conquered a desire to swallow fo-
             cussing on throat. Horribly sleepy.

10:48-11:08 DHARANA, yellow square.
             Battling sleep from start to finish. Managed
             to get a few yellow squares - this time they
             sat on a low, broad, dark pedestal.

Find the stilling of the mind restful and shall surely feel its tonic and invigorating effects later, and somewhere deep within I sense the peace and rest of slipping over the edge. For one second of this rest!

11:15-35   HARPOCRATES.
Babe and blue shell only.
Have a feeling of well being and poise to-night, more in tune. Due to talk of A.C. this evening?

Aug 14
A M
5:55-6:15   ASANA, thunderbolt.
6:15-35   DHARANA, yellow square.
Same difficulties, same accomplishment.
6:40-7:00   HARPOCRATES.
Got hold of this but twice. Could not detach myself from the life around me.
7:58-8:18   PRANAYAMA.
4-8-8-4. Difficult this morning, possibly too near the breakfast hour.

? Have discovered my attitude toward this Abbey is as a stopping place for the night with a moving on in the morning. Why? Because of the extreme contrast of my former life? I do not mean physical but emotional. The pleasurable contacts of the Studio and home circle, the clasped hand, the linked arm, the embrace of friend and friend, cheek against cheek of one more dear, the outpourings and inbreathings of a happy affectional life. I always thought these human contacts necessary for balance. Is this part of the crucifixion of Self. Much can be gained by mastering an empty stomach. I am in darkness, I cannot see ahead. However, the dark is always interesting!
Training of the Mind, in part, by Bennett.
Short nap.
EQUINOX V.
Why this horrible difficulty with the physical?
No. First, 1 day of bleeding piles, at least what I think this, never before having had the same experience I cannot speak with certainty; then soreness of muscles which I attributed to swimming. Now head upset, stomach calling attention to itself, painful to pull myself together after lying down? Intestines moving, sp it cannot result from constipation be poison from that source. I feel sore from centre to circumference.

10:35-45   PRANAYAMA, which I doubt did any good. Conscious of body at every step. Sicilians, 5, about 300

feet from me have been shouting and shrieking
all morning, beating two trees with long
sticks. Head aching. For two days emtional
has been thundering away at my doors. Am I
beginning to feel sorry for myself!

10:50-11:10 ASANA, thunderbolt.
Lost out on swallow.

11:19-30 DHARANA, yellow square.
Somewhat distasteful at the start, but cannot
be compared with distaste of yesterday. Found
myself speculating concerning upset condition,
deciding it was result of swallowing heaps of
salt water.

11:37-12:00 HARPOCRATES.
Fight to continue with this. Finally overcame
this, got as far as babe and shell. However,
Elasticity for the first became a part of me,
I mean, the seed planted. Also thoughts about
ices and ice water.

P M
1:00 In bed. Find it is all a Sicilian fever.

Aug 15
P M
Yesterday afternoon in bed with high fever, up
for breakfast this morning, but feeling quite
faint. Up and down all day, principally down.
Stomach very sore and head troublesome.

Aug 16
P M
My feet are on the ground. I am conscious of
definiteness, a heading toward a certain point,
no more groping, the path is straight. I feel
in a cave slowly emerging toward light.
Has my resolution to be a part of the life
around me brought this about?

Aug 17
6:45 Last night went down to defeat - but out of this
defeat came understanding. Therefore was it
not victory, having to touch bottom to reach
the top?
The devotional part of me must have an outlet -
I starve on Intellect. Remember this.

Aug 18
A.M. 8.00   Understanding of last night corroborated by
             remarks of Beast at breakfast table.

P.M.   My first definite swims, Channel and the Spitz
             - quite tired when getting ashore.

             ¼ Capsule of Grass on return from bath.

             Later: Slight headache.

9:00   Said Pentagram - Shummie and I alone.

Aug 19
A.M.
6:15-35   ASANA, thunderbolt.
6:35-55   DHARANA, yellow square. My mind became one
             with it.
7:05-23   HARPOCRATES.
12:00   ½ Capsule Grass.
             At tiffin, Kubler Khan.
P.M.
4:00   Apparently no result from Grass, unless slight
             headache.

10:12-32   ASANA, thunderbolt.
10:33-53   DHARANA, yellow square. Mind more still than at
             any time heretofore, yellow beautifully
             smooth. While I noticed voices of Lea and
             A.C. they seemed far away and I did not lose
             square. Time dragged.
10:58-11:18 HARPOCRATES.
             Difficult to start, Hansi crying. Did not
             get good visualization.

Aug.20
A.M.
6:05-25   ASANA, thunderbolt.
6:25-45   DHARANA, yellow square.
             Why this docility of mind? It wanders, of
             course, but comes back meekly enough.
             At some time between these exercises and those
             of last night I got a more complete reali-
             zation of mind as an instrument.
6:50-7:12   HARPOCRATES.
             Was seized with repugnance for this at
             start; broke through this feeling once,
             only to have it return again.
P.M.
12:00   Full capsule of Grass.
1:05   A feeling of heaviness in nerves of arms;

slight drowsiness. Lay down but would not permit sleep.

1:23   Sensation on chin: thought my finger was resting there, but no.

1:26   Feeling as though ankles were crossed; but no, lying side by side as I was on my back. Was almost asleep when I noticed this, and XXXX therefore willed myself awake.

After this followed visions of people, country scenes, mountain and one or two marine views - all in monotone of a silver sheen. After this, slept.

10:05-25   ASANA, thunderbolt.

10:25-45   DHARANA, yellow square.
    Negative; both very tedious.

10:46-11:05 HARPOCRATES.
    Was tempted several times to abandon Babe and follow California method of still pool or Space.

Aug.21
A.M.

6:00-20   ASANA, thunderbolt.

6:20-40   DHARANA, yellow square.
    Mind wanders, but nevertheless I am getting a hold on this self-same square.

6:45-7:05   HARPOCRATES.
    I have gained in Dharana, seemingly lost something here. Increasingly difficult to get stillness, also to visualize.

P.M.

9:35-55   ASANA, thunderbolt.

9:55-10: ? DHARANA, yellow square.
    Watch stopped. Think this has become tedious because I am better able to hold sq. Mind not so frequently diverted by other scenes.

10   HARPOCRATES.
    Better to-night; visualization & stillness.

Aug 22
A.M.   Very poor night; little sleep.

5:50-6:10 ASANA, thunderbolt.

6:10-30   DHARANA, yellow square.
    Both stupid.

6:35-53   HARPOCRATES.
    First 10 mins.good, afterwards continually lost vision and one time found myself almost asleep.

P.M.

9:35-55   ASANA, thunderbolt.
    Sleepy before finishing.

9:57-10:17   DHARANA, yellow square.
       I certainly can hold the square better,
       but to-night am quite sleepy.

10:20-40   HARPOCRATES.
       Very tedious; got complete picture. Sleepy.

Aug.23.
A.M.
6:10-30   ASANA, thunderbolt.
       Steady.

6:30-50   DHARANA, yellow square.
       Mind wandered almost as much as two weeks
       ago. However, find I can bring it back with
       less effort and can produce square with less
       waste of time and energy.

6:56-7:16   HARPOCRATES.
P.M.
9:55-10:20   ASANA, thunderbolt.
10:20-40   DHARANA, yellow square.
       For first time got square with physical
       senses shut off - for a wee fraction of
       time. Right elbow extremely painful.

10:45-11:00   HARPOCRATES.
       Tied in knots. Will work for freedom Bou-
       Saada way (lying flat on back).

Aug.24.
P.M.   Experimenting during night in - another body
       shall I say? Physical in restful slumber:
       I was conscious.

6:27-47   ASANA, thunderbolt.
6:47-7:12   DHARANA, yellow square.
       Mind wandering badly.

7:12-30   HARPOCRATES.
       Mind still harping on argument of last
       night regarding 'drugs'.

Aug.25
A.M.   Arrived in Palermo last evening at six and
       went to Hotel des Palmes. Dinner served at
       8:30. Returned to my room at 9:30, prepared
       for bed, intending to read till 10:30 and
       then take up hour's work. Fell asleep.
       When I waked I could not work and slept
       till 7 this a.m. A wonderful night's rest!
       Very refreshing.

7:32-52   ASANA, thunderbolt.
7:52-8:12   DHARANA, yellow square.
       Difficult, as my mind wished to 'chatter',
       and I hiccoughed for 10 minutes.

8:20-35   HARPOCRATES.
       Stopped the 'chattering'; got picture but
       could not get the stillness.

P.M.
9:55-10:15 ASANA, thunderbolt.
10:15-20   DHARANA, yellow square.
          Simply could not work with chattering peo-
          ple, a piano going and the large mastiff
          downstairs barking vociferously. In a hor-
          rible state. May, 1918 I knew I was sane:
          now I am not so sure.

Aug 26.
A.M.
7:50-8:10 ASANA, thunderbolt.
8:10-30   DHARANA, yellow square.
          Dreadful: my mind feels as if in a straight
          jacket.
8:35-52   HARPOCRATES.
          Which was not Harpocrates, but a going after
          the cause of my difficulties. Time and
          again it has been demonstrated that I cannot
          live in the region of the mind - always cha-
          os. Why will I slough back! I stand above
          it: it is a mirror only to reflect to Me
          fragments of the All Mind.
P.M.
10:10-30   ASANA, thunderbolt.
10:30-50   DHARANA, yellow square.
          Mind fussy at start, but subduing it was
          able to turn steady gaze on square.
          Nothing less than God is worthy of God.
10:55-11:15 HARPOCRATES.
          The stillness once more.

          'At first mind consciously directed to yel-
          low square, afterwards the mind flows to-
          ward it; then arises Love, followed by mar-
          riage and the child.' My own off-spring
          in 'Tokio'?

Aug.27
A.M.   Wonderful, restful sleep.
7:10-30   ASANA, thunderbolt.
7:30-50   DHARANA, yellow square.
          Making progress.
7:55-8:12 HARPOCRATES.
          As a whole, Harpocrates, which seemed the
          easier when starting, is now more difficult
          than Dharana: only occasionally can I become
          silent.
10:00   At peace once more - a stillness encircles
          me, I feel in the Egg of Blue, and there
          arises gratitude and love. Realize my re-
          lationship to Cefalu; so physical environ-
          ment there will no longer distress and up-

set me. I was picturing separation, which
I now know would leave an emptiness.

P.M.
10:15-35   ASANA, thunderbolt.
10:35-55   DHARANA, yellow square.
     Think the lateness of the dinner hour af-
     fects my work: I get tired.
11:00-20   HARPOCRATES.
     First 12 mins.good, then so tired I relaxed
     ½ min. and resumed. Last 5 mins. could vis-
     ualize only.

Aug.28
A.M.
7:20-40   ASANA, thunderbolt.
7:40-8:00   DHARANA, yellow square.
     Very difficult.
8:05-25   HARPOCRATES.
     One long fight; visualization but never
     coming really still.

P.M.
10:27-48   ASANA, thunderbolt.
10:48-11:09 DHARANA, yellow square.
     One continuous fight between inner and outer
     vision. Hard to keep going.
11:15-34   HARPOCRATES.
     An unusual degree of stillness. Last four
     mins.could visualize only.
1:00   Tired from the exercises I fell asleep. In
     sleep dreamed my mother opened package I
     brought her, containing three bottles, a one-
     quart, dark green bottle of the usual shape,
     other two smaller, lower and type of stone
     jug. She tasted contents of one bottle and
     said it was most bitter, and I discovered
     the other two were empty. This was an in-
     tense surprise as I was at some pains to
     carry the three.
     During this time I have tossed and pitched
     upon the bed with nerves a-tingle and con-
     scious of solar plexus; never sufficiently
     awake to rouse myself.

Aug.29
A.M.
     After writing the above, said beginning of
     Pentagram and made the Star and Circle. Af-
     terwards slept until seven.
8:05-25   ASANA, thunderbolt.
     Shall do Dharana and Harpocrates at noon;
     head thick.
11:35-58   DHARANA, yellow square.
     Another prolonged fight, mind refusing to be
     directed. One persistent intrusion being

face (principally) and figure of Allan Bennett in an old-world street, with many
people about. At about the same time came
the consciousness that I willed this vision,
saying 'I shall see Allan Bennett'. I mean
by this that the theatrical side of me
saw drama in this and produced it.
Later came Paris, Blvd Raspail, Mrs.Eaton
there, London and Bickie - this last occasioned, no doubt, by receipt of letter
from Bickie this morning.

If dislike be necessary to progress, I
must be making headway of sorts: I abominate
these exercises.

P.M.	
12:00-30	HARPOCRATES.

Dreadful things to be seen and without one
grain of sympathy. The arrogant Ego should
take note.

7:58   Lying on bed thinking of Harpocrates
vision, I saw myself finish climbing out of
a dark chasm, the last bit of the ascent being the emerging from behind what seemed
huge, repulsive bat wings. This chasm of
rock. The way ahead, with slight incline
toward horizon, was entirely over small
rocks of the boulder type, all round, no
sharp edges, and over this way streamed a
white radiance. Toward the source of this
radiance I moved without once looking back.

11:55   Spent the evening with Mr Bush, whom I found
entertaining. Yet am I so tired I shall
retire without work.

Aug 30
A.M.
7:53-8:18   ASANA, thunderbolt.
8:13-33   DHARANA, yellow square.
            Better than yesterday.
8:40-9:00   HARPOCRATES.
            Chaotic.

P.M.
10:22-42   ASANA, thunderbolt.
10:42-11:02 DHARANA, yellow square.
            Tedious throughout.
11:07-22   HARPOCRATES.
            Visualized, but no stillness. Could not
            eliminate voices outside my door.

Aug.31
A.M.
7:02-22   ASANA, thunderbolt.

7:22-40   DHARANA, yellow square.
               For first time, felt as if I were regarding
               square with entire body.

7:45-8:05   HARPOCRATES.
               Very broken.

P.M.

               Returned to Cefalu.

Sept. 1
A.M.   Retired last night without exercises, but
               could not sleep. Finally lit lamp and took
               Book of Lies. At 2:45 turned out light and
               finally slept, though fitfully.
               This seemed a physical condition as spirit
               and mind were calm. Nerves tight and seemed
               to have a life of their own, which was wide
               awake.

6:37-57   ASANA, thunderbolt.
              DHARANA, yellow square.
               Merely a tame asana.

6:57-7:20   HARPOCRATES.
               Ditto. The deeper part of me entirely
               lacking·

P.M.
10:18-38   ASANA, thunderbolt.
10:38-58   DHARANA, yellow square.
               Got hold of sq. Weak toward end.
             HARPOCRATES.
               Invocation, Equinox, Vol III, p 274

               Book of The Law until 12.

Sept. 2
A.M.
4:30   Slept till 2:45
              Book of The Law.

7:43-8:03   ASANA, thunderbolt.
8:03-23   DHARANA, yellow square.
               Held at times, but not at all fresh.
             HARPOCRATES.
               Invocation.

P.M.
10:00-20   ASANA, thunderbolt.
10:20-40   DHARANA, yellow square.
               Difficult, but hung on: mind trying to di-
               vert itself by other, familiar scenes.
             HARPOCRATES.
               Invocation. More and more beautiful as I
               repeat the words.

Sept. 3
A.M.
7:25   Slept until about 2. Disturbance waked me; did
               not sleep again till after 4. Find I am

```
                        now tired enough to be peevish. Boys, too,
                        waked up peevish and crying.
7:30-50   ASANA, thunderbolt.
7:50-8:10 DHARANA, yellow square.
                        Poor. Conflicting emotions about, being
                        tired they found an entrance.
                        HARPOCRATES.
                        Invocation.
P.M.
10:07-27            ASANA, thunderbolt.
10:27-58            DHARANA, yellow square.
                        Held on fairly well; difficult last 5 mins.
                        HARPOCRATES.
                        Invocation.
                        Am beginning to feel the power of certain
                        words read in Equinox - the creative power.
Sept.4
A.M.
10:03-23            ASANA, thunderbolt.
10:23-43            DHARANA, yellow square.
                        For the first time mind was so directed
                        that exercise was reposeful to it - a
                        calming, stilling and strengthening action.
                        HARPOCRATES.
                        Invocation.
                        Power is flowing into me - a storing of
                        the batteries?

Sept.5
A.M.
7:37-57            ASANA, thunderbolt.
7:57-8:13          DHARANA, yellow square.
                        Five mins. short. Got along well for 10 mins.
                        then could not shut off discussion about
                        cow's milk and Poupee.
                        HARPOCRATES.
                        Invocation.

                        Went to pieces at 'Fives'.  This tired me com-
                        pletely.  Why this sudden tempest?

11:27              In a relaxed condition - a letting go all
                        along the line.  Is this because of the
                        Force of which I was conscious for 2 days
                        and which kept me wakeful for 2 nights -
                        the physical not equal to the strain of
                        these stronger vibrations?  Like the labour
                        pains of motherhood, followed in each in-
                        stance by a period of rest?
                        Or, is it astrological?
P.M.
9:18-40            ASANA, thunderbolt.
9:40-10:00         DHARANA, yellow square.
```

My fight with Dharana lies principally
in the last 10 mins., though now finished
last 5 mins fair.

10:10-20　　HARPOCRATES.
　　　　Invocation, preceded by beginning of Pen-
　　　　tagram. When beginning this I entered a
　　　　Temple more vast and silent than any hereto-
　　　　fore conceived. I seemed the size of an in-
　　　　sect in comparison. Was conscious of two
　　　　large pillars to the right and left, to the
　　　　front of which I stood and back of which I
　　　　knew there to be an altar, though shrouded
　　　　in darkness. At one time was conscious of
　　　　lapis blue in this darkness and the word
　　　　Ocelli occurred to me while here.
　　　　After Invocation was finished I willed my-
　　　　self into this Temple and asked for en-
　　　　lightenment, but received nothing.

Sept.6
A.M.
　　　　Waked at 1:30, fussed around trying to sleep,
　　　　dozed a bit, finally read Theocritus, turned
　　　　out light at 4 and slept till 6:12.

6:15+35　　ASANA, thunderbolt.
　　　　So sleepy I ached.

6:35-55　　DHARANA, yellow square.
　　　　Poor.

　　　　HARPOCRATES.
　　　　Beginning of Pentagram, followed by Invoc-
　　　　ation.

P.M.
12:30　　Again away from Love, and when the thumb
　　　　screws are tightened that I may realize
　　　　I am asleep I whimper!

　　　　At Palermo - Mellin's Food for Poupee.

10:30-50　　ASANA, thunderbolt.
10:50-11-10 DHARANA, yellow square.
　　　　Never was so alert before, result of A.C.'s
　　　　enlightening talk concerning Asana. Can
　　　　readily see this method is infinitely bet-
　　　　ter than what I was doing.

　　　　HARPOCRATES.
　　　　Could not remember the entire Invocation.

Sept.7
A.M.
7:20-40　　ASANA, thunderbolt.
7:40-8:00　DHARANA, yellow square.
　　　　This 'poised ready to spring' attitude will
　　　　tone up entire physical and therefore the
　　　　ascending scale of my being. Am most grate-
　　　　ful to be set straight.
　　　　Tired after the above, so rested 10 mins. and
　　　　did what I could of Harpocrates.

P.M. Cefalu.
    Bathing, and swam around a rock, from one beach
     to another, A.C. going ahead, showing me the
     way, selecting resting places. I wish I could
     put into words all that I saw in this action.
     I looked down long vistas and viewed Life
     from many angles.

    Beast has somewhat to do with America.
    Interesting. Sept.28, 1917. Magnolia Ave.

10:45-11:05 ASANA, thunderbolt.
11:05-25 DHARANA, yellow square.
     Rather ragged in spots.
    HARPOCRATES.
     Invocation.

Sept. 8
A.M.
6:10-30 ASANA, thunderbolt.
6:30-50 DHARANA, yellow square.
     Beginning dreadful; toned up somewhat on
     last 10 mins.
    HARPOCRATES.
     Invocation.
     A feeling of inharmony this morning.
10:30 Suppose I should record my dream of last night,
     I have so few.
    In a room with many draperies, another woman
    with me. She showed signs of great agita-
    tion, finally fear and partial collapse.
    Understood 'supernatural' was cause, and
    learned it was a something issuing from the
    top of my head. Three men were called. By
    this time we were in a larger place. They
    too, saw what the woman saw and desired to
    make notes and a reproduction - the latter
    to appear in a 'Sunday Supplement'? 'You
    will become famous' said one, and I waked.
    Should state I felt no uneasiness or fear,
    accepting their statement as true as it was
    something with which I was all ready.familiar

11:05 Tired, I lay down hoping for a few minutes
    sleep. The thought came to enter my Temple
    for rest. (I say 'my' as I have met none
    else there) I did so, remaining for atime
    in front of the pillars. Then I went on to
    the altar, still in darkness, and sank at
    the foot of it. After a time I rose and
    saw lapis draperies fringed with gold. I
    placed my palms on the altar and with tears
    brimming over, repeated: 'I'm home! I'm
    home!'

Think this all right - no emotional reaction:
a feeling of placement, strength and a re-
lease from the 'binding' of others.

10:10-25 PRANAYAMA.
Most vigorous so far, 4-8-8-4.

P.M.
10:10 During Pentragram by A.C. I entered Temple and
found, some distance above my head, that it
was filled with billows of colors, mingling
and intermingling - orderly, beautiful.

10:15-35 ASANA, thunderbolt.
10:35-55 DHARANA, yellow.
I am grateful for the proximity of the Master.
Am very happy to-night.
HARPOCRATES.
Invocation.

Sept. 9
A.M.
6:45-7:05 ASANA, thunderbolt.
Find I can do this better with a mental picture
so have been holding leafNstrewn forest, alert
for the slightest stir of an autumn leaf.

7:10-30 DHARANA, yellow square.
Not as good as Asana - mind sought diversion,
being tired I suppose.
HARPOCRATES.
Invocation.

P.M.
10:10-30 ASANA, thunderbolt.
Made myself flaming body guarding entrance
to Temple.

10:30-50 DHARANA, yellow square.
Last evening and this, when whole being was
centred on square, had a feeling that with
but a slightly deeper concentration Love
would enfold me.
Have noticed with this alertness body becomes moist, at times perspiration trickling
down.
HARPOCRATES.
Invocation & silence.

Sept. 10
A.M. A wonderful sleep.
7:25-55 ASANA, thunderbolt.
Again flaming body guarding Temple; became
intensely active in entire body, which was
set. Last 5 mins. strongly conscious of
I-Amness. Noticed focus was in right side
of body. So frequently it is in left.

7:57-8:17 DHARANA, yellow square.
This suffered because of energy of Asana.

Held to it, however, but there was not the
vigor of last evening. Desire to quit after 15 mins.
HARPOCRATES.
Invocation.

11:00 The feeling of placement which the Temple has
given me continues to fill me with wonder.
Constantly at my back stands that power and
support to keep me calm, inwardly at least.

11:50 Have been going over Book of The Law. See
' .. the blue and gold are seen of the
seeing.' Part I, 60. What shade of blue?

P.M.
4:00 On hill for a rest. Did I get a disappointment
for A.C? Mailed to him in Naples, whither
he has gone, a letter from Russell. Is R.
not coming?
Emptied self, lay still and breathed deeply
for a time, easily, rythmically.

10:15-35 ASANA, thunderbolt.
On guard at Temple door, watching, listening
into Space.

10:35-55 DHARANA, yellow square.
Broke physical once, after 10 mins. Body
moist with perspiration.
HARPOCRATES.
Invocation.

Sept. 11
A.M.
7:15-25 ASANA, thunderbolt.
Poor.

7:15-52 DHARANA, yellow square.
Tied in knots and unable to smooth and thus
free - a rigidity of mind.
HARPOCRATES.
Invocation.

P.M.
10:47 All day I have been conscious of - what?
Something at present undefinable. A physical
fitness, a spiritual nearness, or an enfolding presence. Found myself singing and expressing a feeling of warmth toward objective
life.

10:50-11:10 ASANA, thunderbolt.
Nothing to my credit.
In California, feeling as I do now, I would
have rested the mind a day or two. Shall I
do so here, meantime keeping poised in God?
There is a mental rigidity which I can only
eliminate through rest. Yes - no Dharana.

HARPOCRATES.
　　Invocation.

Sept.12
A.M.
7:10　　　　Wakeful and now so sleepy.　O dear!
7:12-30　　ASANA, thunderbolt.
7:30-50　　DHARANA, yellow square.
　　　　　　Both poor. Due to physical unfitness?
　　　　　　Hardly: mental rigidity continues.
　　　　　HARPOCRATES.
　　　　　　Invocation, and Silence.

P.M.
10:10-20　HARPOCRATES.
　　　　　　Invocation.
10:20-40　ASANA, thunderbolt.
　　　　　　Strong = Space & Silence - a feeling that
　　　　　　could I encompass but a trifle more I would
　　　　　　spread out and become Silence and so rid
　　　　　　myself of this intellectual concept.
10:40-11:00　DHARANA, yellow square.
　　　　　　This suffered somewhat from Asana.

　　　　　　This time focus seemed in left.

　　　　　　This method of concentration seems a lift-
　　　　　　ing of one's self by the boot-straps. Per-
　　　　　　spiring: left leg painful.

Sept.13
A.M.　　　Wakened several times by Hansi's audible
　　　　　　dreaming.　Assume I am not in deep slumber
　　　　　　or this would not happen.
7:10　　　HARPOCRATES.
　　　　　　Invocation.
7:20-40　ASANA, thunderbolt.
　　　　　　Nothing worthwhile.
7:40-8:00　DHARANA, yellow square.
　　　　　　Could not get mind working properly at any
　　　　　　time.　Left thigh became troublesome after
　　　　　　5 mins. By 10 I was in agony. For 5 mhs.
　　　　　　struggled to continue - last 5 tried des-
　　　　　　perately to get square, hoping thereby to
　　　　　　eliminate pain. Had to lie down to rest af-
　　　　　　terward. It seemed the core, the life of
P.M.　　　the thigh - and I was about gasping.
　　　　　Afternoon, lying down.
　　　　　　Came remembrance of Asana held by me at
　　　　　　sanitarium May, 1918, when suffering in-
　　　　　　tensely after a very prolonged holding
　　　　　　came voice:'God does not inflict pain.'

10:40-11:00　ASANA,
　　　　　　Fussed around trying Cal.Asana 10 mins.
　　　　　　then returned to thunderbolt: so finished.

```
11:00-18    DHARANA, yellow sq.
                Started out with a strength that surprised
                me; tired before finishing and so lost
                somewhat.
            HARPOCRATES.
                Invocation.
Setp.14
A.M.            Slept well.
7:20-40     ASANA, thunderbolt.
                No alertness at all.
7:40-56     DHARANA, yellow sq.
                Mind tight: cannot get control.
7:56-8:10   HARPOCRATES.
                Invocation and silence.  This helped
                smooth me. Must use it first.
P. M.
10:08-28    ASANA, thunderbolt.
                Alert in Space: held this fairly well.
10:30-49    DHARANA, yellow sq.
                Difficulty in producing sq. Broke after
                10 mins, to kill mosquito!  Could not re-
                cover again. Fight to continue. Left leg
                paining, then it went 'asleep' and after
                became numb.
            HARPOCRATES.
                Invocation.
Sept.15
A.M.           A good night.
7:30-50     ASANA, thunderbolt.
                Poor.
7:50-8-10   DHARANA, yellow sq.
                Difficulty at start, sq.hard to visualize,
                but afterwards settled into an inward poise.
                Always know when channels are free by deep,
                full and regular breathing.
            HARPOCRATES.
                Invocation.
P.M.
4:00        Shummie read 'Across The Gulf' while I painted
                floor.  It occurs to me that one with a
                knowledge of past incarnations might enjoy
                adopting at intervals some part of a former
                apparel.  This accounting for what - to an
                American mind at least,- might be taken as
                an eccentricity in the dress at times of
                A.C.
            Also, would this account for a certain deep
                blue heavy silk robe I picture for myself.
                Have I at some time worn such, open at the
                throat and breast, showing beneath a slip
                of - not white, not cream; I do not get
                this now; but I always thought it was white.
                Now I know it is not.
```

10:20-40   ASANA, thunderbolt.
        Have decided that I am attempting to wade
        around in the wrong fields. Asana pertains
        to the physical: I have been trying to reach
        - what? Something beyond Dharana it seems.

10:40-11:00 DHARANA, yellow sq.
        Got sq.again and results first 10 mins.,
        then mind wandered flagrantly.
        HARPOCRATES.
        Invocation.

Sept.16
A.M.
7:20-30   HARPOCRATES.
        Invocation.

7:30-50   ASANA, thunderbolt.
        Snarled up between tight breath and a con-
        sequent holding of top of stomach, producing
        a caved in feeling and inability to take
        a good breath.

7:50-8:10   DHARANA, yellow sq.
        Hit this well at times - mind wandering
        badly at others.

P.M.
9:20   See in Eq V, p 98 - '2.The Ego; that which
        thinks 'I' - a falsehood, because to think
        'I' is to deny 'Not-I' and thus to create
        the Dyad.'
        Harpocrates: Behold I am.
        My entry of Sept.10. Watch this and see just
        what 'I am' means to me.

9:45-10:05 ASANA, thunderbolt.
        Got down to earth. Held myself a runner
        ready to spring over the line at the signal.
        Held this steady - in the beginning at
        least, but it took strength; rested a mo-
        ment for Dharana.

10:06-25   DHARANA, yellow sq.
        Kept my head in sight of earth here too.
        Tired after 10 mins. Difficulty in holding
        sq. so grabbed it between hands and held so
        for 5 mins, using an extra spurt of strength.
        Relaxed a moment, then finished tamely.
        Left leg numb, no feeling in foot.

10:30   HARPOCRATES.
        Invocation.

Sept.17
A.M.
7:22-42   ASANA, thunderbolt. Again a runner. Later came restriction of
        upper part of stomach region. Willed 'I
        am' consciousness to spot & breathed deeply
        and regularly against it, which made throat
        feel as though used incorrectly in reading
        aloud.

7:42-8:00   DHARANA, yellow sq.
> Started yellow sq but stopped and wentafter
> stomach. Discovered I was holding it; gave
> release and with that came more stature -
> as though pressure had been removed from a
> young shoot and that it then straightened &
> shot upwards. Expansion & freedom in throat
> especially right side, up across right eye
> and into right lobe.

This spot has troubled me time & again in Cal.
> Once there was a fine relief which I seemed
> to breathe consciously from between shoulders.

HARPOCRATES.
> Invocation.

P.M.
10:25-55   ASANA, thunderbolt.
> Used too much strength on this.
> Will take this up on hill, when I have time
> to go.

10:55-11:15 DHARANA, yellow sq.
> Got well into this, for 15 mins. Then leg in
> such torture I moved it and returned to
> work.
> Is not the perfection of concentration in
> dropping & taking up at will a subject-
> starting again where one leaves off? C.B.
> DeMille who, in any conversation having a
> definite end in view, can stop at a point
> selected by himself, lead his hearers through
> a labyrinth and return to the identical com-
> ma and continue. To what extent can this
> concentration & memory be carried?
> In holding sq noticed I breathe deeply &
> fully thro left nostril, breath at times seem-
> ing to flow into head, which I found invigo-
> rating.

HARPOCRATES.
> Invocation.

Sept.18
A.M.
7:30-50   ASANA.
> Thunderbolt at start: afterwards modified
> as an experiment.

7:50-8:10   DHARANA, yellow sq.
> Difficulty in holding sq. Breath thro right
> nostril but not so effective as breath of
> last night.
> Leg numb & lifeless.

HARPOCRATES.
> Invocation.

M

Another Sept.6 day - shall I ever get away
> from thinking of self! I am very tired.

P.M.
4:00   Reading 'Scented Garden of Abdullah'. Letter
       of Carey rather interesting, though a rep-
       etition of what I have seen elsewhere.
       Have often wondered why I am not a homo-
       sexualist, as the society of women means
   ✓   more to me than that of men - they stimu-
       late, I was about to say my mind, but per-
       haps that is the effect. I enjoy the phy-
       sical contact of women I love. Then, too.
       amorous advances of men repel me, they seem
       rude and crude, lacking in delicacy.

5:00   On hill trying to straighten myself, but Nature
       give me nothing because I myself give
       nothing.
       Demons seem to possess me: I feel insane
       at times.

10:15-35   ASANA.
           Nothing satisfactory.
10:35-55   DHARANA, yellow sq.
           Good to-night. of course, lost many times,
           but could set up again without loss of
           much time & energy.
           Breath left nostril, full & deep.
           HARPOCRATES.
           Invocation.

11:08   I am thinking about results - watching myself,
        criticizing myself. This must stop! Storm
        or peace, love or hate - let either come
        or go. But my whole being goes into hate
        as it does into whatever I do!

Sept. 19
A.M.
7:30-50   ASANA.
          N.G.
7:50-8:10   DHARARA, yellow sq.
            Held this rather well for morning.
            Breath through right nostril.
            HARPOCRATES.
            Invocation.

10:45   On hill. Mever was wind through trees morese-
        ductive, but I put it from me.
        Inwardly I feel impotent. This A.M. I take
        hold with baby fingers, and yet I have stood
   ℥   apart, and with strength. Was this strength
        given by another to show me the way. Every-
        thing is in such a muddle!
        These feelings, against no one in particular,
        that flood my being and at times rise to

2
an impotent rage so that I could grind under
my heel this Abbey and all of its inmates
(and I just this moment hurt an ant & am sorry) are cumulative. They mount and mount, until not finding an outlet they bowl me over
and find such outlet through my collapse.

P.M.
10:10-30   ASANA.
              Got something here.
10:30-49   DHARANA, yellow sq.
              Wish I could see inside & know just what
              is taking place. Regarded sq in 2 differ-
              ent ways. Which is proper? One requires
              more of me than the other. Shall try this
              again.

Sept.20.
A.M.
7:17-40   ASANA.
              Started as runner, poised for start. Later
              changed to ready to leap across deep flow-
              ing water to end of small, narrow spring
              board.
7:40-58   DHARANA, yellow sq.
              Started out as usual, noticed breath in
              right nostril. Decided on what I noticed
               last night. Breath deeper nor did I notice
    √   from which nostril, but did notice that the
              breath seemed to spray up the spine from
              just below center of shoulder to and into
              lower part of head. This always produces a
              feeling of well being.

P.M.
4:00   I feel inexpressibly bored and yet there seems
            rebellion. How can this be? I wished to
            write Mary K but would not pay her so small
            a compliment. I sew a bit and toss that
            aside, go to the hill and return. These
            bawling children!
            And I find Shummie feeling as I do and realize
            my selfishness. There is kinship here -
            what? I believe I knew her long ago and
            that is why I was surprised when seeing her
            on my arrival. Was it Paris or Rome? I
            understand her, the heart of the woman,
            and with understanding comes Love.

10:10-30   ASANA.
              Tol'able.
10:30-50   DHARANA, yellow sq.
              Mind wandering constantly.
            HARPOCRATES.
              Invocation.

Sept.

Sept.21
A.M.
6:35-50   ASANA`
        Bum
6:50-7:10 DHARANA, yellow sq.
        N G
     HARPOCRATES.
      Invocation.

P.M.
9:15-35   ABANA.
      Too sleepy.
      Tried studying Eg.to wake myself.
     HARPOCRATES.
      Invocation.
10:00-10 DHARANA, yellow sq.
      One yawn after another - yawns of mind not
      of body. Shall sleep; if I wake during
      night shall try.

Sept.22
A.M.
4:40   What did I receive? First in the soul? I was
      conscious of receiving something through feel-
      ing and drew near enough physical-waking to
      hear myself mention 'soul'. Second had to do
      with mind. This was more clear but I could
      not bring anything through.
4:50-5:07   Settled myself for Dharana but all doors
      closed. If I could understand this cutting
      off! The intellect, yes; but at times there
      is something else - I know the physical lo-
      cation in the head. Last night I could not
      visualize because of this, nor now. There is
      a definite obstruction.

7:30   I sit for work, but utterly impossible.

Noon.   While at bath came question of open mind.
      Have always insisted there should be no cmn-
      victions, that all messages given the world
      were definitely arranged by the gods to meet
      every individual, many gates being required to
      the kingdom of heaven. But that does not
      mean, of course, that we should not have the
      utmost confidence in our method it means only
      that the other fellow, though entirely opposed
      many be absolutely right, considering the present
      growth of that individual· But I should not "
      have to argue this out - it is all together
      too plain.

P.M.
2:30   I am still in the muddle and cannot understand
      it at all. I feel no self-reliance: a pawn
      moved at the will of another - I mean, inwardly.

My mind is quite beyond my grasp and I find
this tiring. I say 'neither pleasure nor
pain' and yet at times my spirit droops: I
cannot put from me the question of responsibility for the condition.

4:10   After writing above took 'Stolen Post Office'
and came to hill. Worked on several pages
and then slept.

10:30- 5   ASANA.
       Still blank. There is nothing I can grasp.
       The mind feels like the throat expanded,
       held tight and drowsy as when one yawns.
       I never willed vision before coming to Cefa-
       lu so cannot say whether I have experienced
       just this condition before.
       All this reacts on the physical, leaving
       me weary in body.

Srpt.23
A.M.   In first sleep of last night there was a
       slipping of me from Me - or was it Me from
       me?
6:00-15   Tried to locate difficulty of present condition.
       N G
5:15-35   ASANA.
       A sitting still.
6:40-7:00   DHARANA, yellow sq.
       Perhaps I saw sq for period of 1 min -
       perhaps 3.

This A.M. I am filled with resentment. What
shall be the next mood? Last evening on the
court in the moonlight I was quiet enough but
no mind was there, though fragments of conversation flitted quietly through. This morning
all thought brings emotional reaction.
    All this may be 'dryness' but certainly un-
like anything ever experienced before, when I
felt like a deserted house with flapping doors
& windows. But this is not emptiness; it is
a something cut off in the centre of my head,
an inability to direct thought.

There is no doubt at all in my mind that Shummie is part of the plan; therefore why all this
harpooning. Poor devil!
    I reckon a big fault of mine has been, &
still is, expecting too much.

Why 'fear' in these invocations, though I assume instilling fear is not meant. I can understand hate: let them hate, but fear ---?

Started Harpocrates but could not continue
with nothing to give. So feeling the need
of some action went under instead.

10:00
A cable from 666. Did I detect a note of
loneliness in myself? Is the wobbly pupil
looking for strength from the Master? Fee
Wah, when I called for him under somewhat
similar circumstances, came with the simple
statement: 'You must go to God, not to me.'
(When mentioning Fee Wah I always gurgle.
I detect a note of justification. As if he
needed that! I seem, too, to feel him smile.)

'That I will rely only on myself.'
Just what does this mean? Here is where I am
at a loss regarding the use of artificial
stimulants for the accomplishment of a definite work.

P.M.
After dinner Shummie and I sat on the court
till nine o'clock. A brilliant moon - very
illuminating! Then we came in and read Return of Agamemnon!

10:30-50 ASANA.
10:50-11:10 DHARANA, yellow sq.
    Something, but little. However, no re-
    action. I feel calm.
HARPOCRATES.
    Invocation. Thank God I can go through
    it to-night.

Sept.24
A.M.
After first sleep of exhaustion, waked, near
3 and slept not till almost six, when I fell
asleep to dream I was seated in a large dining hall, at a small table against the wall.
A man came to my table, taking chair opposite
me, piling papers and cap against wall. I
was surprised as the room was empty and I
looked enquiringly at the head-waiter. He
paid no attention. The seated man suddenly
had a friend by his side and this man he placed at the end of the table, facing the wall.
I rose & picking up my dishes said sarcastic-
ally: 'Gentlemen, permit me to present you
the only table in the room' (Not exact words
but something to that effect). Catching eye
of headwaiter directed at first man with a
knowing smile, I turned back and hurled my
dishes squarely in the middle of the table
smashing everything in sight. They looked
blank amazement and incredulity. I laughed.

```
7:20-8:00    ASANA.
8:00-8:20    DHARANA, yellow sq.
                 Same story.
                 I am tired.

 10:00
             At 9:30 prepared for beach but could not find
             boys any place. Returned to house and took
             'World's Tragedy' and came to hill. I need
             enlightenment on 'perversion' - a something
             abhorrent when viewed from the personal stand-
             point.
                 Where do I belong?  I want mental stimula-
             tion - not physical.  Thank heaven neither dirty
             literature nor obscene pictures stir me: I can
             read the one and look at the other when artistic
             and of merit.  But how is the mental approached?

10:42-57     PRANAYAMA. 4-8-8-4

P.M.         Found Lea home on my return.

10:37        ASANA.
                 In the saddle once more. Did not need to vis-
             ualize to keep body alert.
10:57-11:20  DHARANA, yellow sq.
                 To-day longed for mental marriage, furrows
             ploughed deep in this mind of mine.  Behold,
             a little honeymoon to-night and the landscape
             seems more fair.
                 (Query: Am I an hermaphrodite!)
             HARPOCRATES.
                 Invocation.
Sept.25
A.M.
5:47-6:08    ASANA`
                 Mind held forth on various arguments:
             1. With God living in the heart, radiating
             out to all, the proper word on the lips at
             the proper time, does one need to shout Him
             from the house-tops.
             2. Which, to the average onlooker, are the
             more convincing - the freak; or the one who,
             through a splendid conviction and in God-
             inspired simplicity, puts aside years of
             conventionality, traditions born and bred in
             the bone and who therefore stands in a fine
             serenity?
6:08-30      DHARANA, yellow sq.
                 Difficult to visualize at first, then found
             myself taking hold with the 'baby fingers',
             though strengthened somewhat now.
                 I see I have not entered in diary an ex-
```

perience of last fall of becoming conscious,
just after the stilling of objective before
sleep, in a body of great majesty and poise.
Was that the spiritual? Is this the spiritual
now endeavoring to reach through? With it
comes poise, the impersonal, and a consciousness of life above all this petty turmoil -
which at times seems so gigantic.

P.M.
2:30

I come up here on hill, stagger and fall, And
sob and sob violently for almost an hour
because ~~that I~~
I am shaken to the core. It comes thick
and fast!

9:45-10:05   ASANA.
                    N G
10:05-23   DHARANA, yellow sq.
                    Too weary in mind and spirit to do anything.
                HARPOCRATES.
                    Invocation.

Sept.26
A.M.
6:20-40   ASANA.
                    A sitting still.
6:40-6:58   DHARANA, yellow sq.
                    A sitting still.
                HARPOCRATES.
                    Invocation.

Walked far up the mountains, leaving at ten.
I walked something out - my first liking of
these Cefalu hills. Returned at one.

10:05-25   ASANA.
                    Fair.
10:25-43   DHARANA, yellow sq.
                    What is this in lower back of skull? This
                    evening I regarded sq with that part of me;
                    consciousness focussed there: difficult but
                    satisfying. Had to rest after 10 mins and
                    use brain section first used in this vis-
                    ualization.
                        It must be important, else why the work
                    going on there during the past year?
                HARPOCRATES.
                    Invocation.

Sept.27
A.M.

Between waking and sleeping state, sometime
during the night, discovered some inner part
of me moaning in great agony. Moan became
sufficiently audible for one standing close
by to have heard. Remember now this occurred
once before - when? And is it soul or spirit?

```
6:25-45      ASANA.
             Fair.
6:45-7:05    DHARANA, yellow sq.
             Taking hold with this newer center in head, I
             seem to be at the beginning once more, but am
             quite sure this is the larger, better way.
             HARPOCRATES.
             Invocation.

10:00        Hill.  The Red Star.
10:48-11:03  PRANAYAMA.  4-8-8-4
P.M.
10:10-30     ASANA.
             Mind going like a whirligig over something new,
             out of which Lea comes with vine leaves in her
             hair.
             Now I have both adjusted.
10:30-45     DHARANA, yellow sq.
             Ditto.
             HARPOCRATES.
             Invocation.

Sept.28
A.M.         In such heavenly deep sleep last night, yet twice
             did I come to the waking state, leaving my
             body aching for sleep.  Why is this?

7:40-8:00    ASANA.
             N G
8:00-20      DHARANA, yellow sq.
             At intervals only.
             HARPOCRATES.
             Invocation.

             These maids of the vine leaves produce in me much
             levity.  I see the humorous side of this Abbey
             and feel quite frivolous.  O, for my pen!
P.M.
3:30         Hill.  Some demon has departed.  I look around me
             and wonder how I could have suffered so acute-
             ly.  It seems incredible!
             Now I float, idly, with the stream.

9:45-10:05   ASANA.
             Alert.
10:05-25     DHARANA, yellow sq.
             Still in starting period.
             HARPOCRATES.
             Invocation.

Sept.29
A.M.
6:25-45      ASANA.
             Alert, tho improperly done: balance wrong &
             could not locate difficulty.  Can do this bet-
             ter with vision, but then it ceases to be ASana.
```

6:45-7:04   DHARANA, yellow sq.
       A calm, high-mindedness, suggesting a cool pur-
       ity. (Does this mean singleness of purpose?)
       HARPOCRATES.
       Invocation.
       Prayer and thanksgiving.

11:15   A special letter to Mary K.

12:00   The feeling of an approaching doom. Silly.
P.M.

3:07   Hill.
       Strange. I lie here, idly, drifting with the pass-
       ing clouds, when there floats across my conscious-
       ness as a cloud, the following:
       A clasping of arms, lip against lip, a spinning out
       into Space, myself resting in his bosom; he mount-
       ing higher & higher, but always the cloud, al-
       ways an obscuring film. I negative, inactive,
       absorbing only, a burden.
       Then came realization of bi-sexual nature of both,
       the necessity for the masculine from me. With
       this came awakening and clarity, the realization
       that both natures of the individual must be si-
       multaneously roused for surpassing spiritual in-
       sight, for a conscious merging of Souls in ec-
       stacy beyond comprehension.
       But for this I need more growth.
       (N.B. This a distinct improvement over Lone Pine,
       where negative side only was grasped and that
       through copulation. But at that time there was
       a sex strain, which no doubt colored the picture.
       How thoroughly impersonal one must be for the
       vision. This is something to think of, as there
       must still be the personal. For, after all, may
       this not refer to my merging with Space, the
       breaking up of the walls of individuality and the
       flowing out into the 'Sea of Nothingness'?)

       Feeling all in, went to bed immediately after dinner.

Sept.30
A.M.   Wakeful, more or less, waked at 5:45 and got up,
       and went out doors for a time.

6:20-40   ASANA.
       That caved-in feeling of stomach. What causes
       it? Could do no work as I cannot breathe, though
       held posture. What is this suppression?

6:40-7:00   DHARANA, yellow sq.
       A confused surge of thoughts.
       Am I full of astral fumes? Head thick.
       HARPOCRATES.
       Invocation.

P.M.

You are missing the planes.

P.M.   A.C. back from Naples.

6:00   'I want to be the greatest - that is genius'.
                          Does this leave all channels free for the
                          Divine influx necessary for the genius?

10:05   Funny about my dream of Sept.24, that it should
                             precede.
                          This evening I ask A.C. a simple question. For
                             answer he smiles the same head-waiter smile
                             at Lea. Not having any plates to smash and
                             thus eliminate my irritation, I remain peeved.

10:20-40   ASANA.
               Poor.
10:40-58   DHARANA, yellow sq.
               Ditto.
            HARPOCRATES.
               Invocation.

Oct.1
A.M.
6:20-40   ASANA
6:40-7:00   DHARANA, yellow sq.
               No control.
            HARPOCRATES.
               Invocation and Silence.

Noon.   Restless, I want to get away and onto the hill.
                             And I hang around waiting for food!

8:45-9:05   ASANA.
9:05-25   DHARANA, yellow sq.
               Neither satisfactory. Mind hopping about.
            HARPOCRATES.
               Invocation.

Oct.2
A.M.   (Written 3)
                          Why no entries, especially for A.M., as I did my
                             usual morning work?

                          Moved across the hill. A strange feeling of ex-
                             haustion, which I attribute to using the broom
                             too strenuously, being unaccustomed to such work.
P.M.

                          Set up my altar in the West, consecrating it and
                             myself in a feeble attempt at Magic of my own.

                          After Pentagram in Abbey, returned to new abode at
                             8:15. Talked with Shummie till 11, afterwards
                             we sat in the moon-light long, then took blank-
                             ets and slept on the hill.
                          Top of head paining at intervals during night.

Oct.3
A.M.   Again no entries, though I worked, but remember

it was unsuccessful, as a whole.

P.M.
    HARPOCRATES.
      At altar. Shall always do this way.

9:25-35   ASANA.
      Good - without vision, tho at beginning I did
      think of alertness of Fox terrier.

9:45-10:05 DHARANA, yellow sq & purple egg.
      Being new, I had no difficulty in visualizing.
      Tho should add my mind has been in good condi-
      tion (for me.) all evening.
      First impression egg touched the four sides of
      sq, therefore not an oval - good yellow, good
      purple, though yellow smoother in texture.
      Tried to make egg small; very difficult and
      color not so brilliant.
      After fifteen minutes found myself tiring.

Oct.4
A.M.
    HARPOCRATES.
      Invocation.

6:25-45   ASANA.
      For morning, good. If and when I conquer morn-
      ing, shall I have the day conquered?

6:45-7:05 DHARANA, yellow sq- purple egg.
      Same report here, good. Lower corners not as good
      a color. In reading most people read upper part
      of letters only. Does this account for lack of
      color in lower corners?

P.M.
    HARPOCRATES.
      Invocation.

10:00-15   ASANA.
      Good alertness.

10:20-40   DHARANA, yellow sq & purple egg.
      Satisfactory. In beginning mind hopped about.
      One thing I remember,- I was 'casting' Spiriteer,
      selecting Edith Chapman for the role of medium.

Oct.5
A.M.

    HARPOCRATES.
      Invocation. Achievement first.

6:10-30   ASANA.
      Not satisfactory.

6:30-48   DHARANA, yellow sq & purple egg.
      Tried to make egg flat like square, succeeded.
      Concentration not forced, mind relaxed and flow-
      ing, I contacted another spot! Were my head sev-
      ered near base of skull, would say it was that
      end of spinal cord left exposed.

    Italian lesson.

    That peculiar all-gone feeling in region of diaphragm
      of Oct.2.

9:55-10:01   PRANAYAMA in Asana.

               Now plan to make this and Italian a part of my
               morning work, - that is, before 10.

P.M.   Top of head, off and on, for possibly 2 hours.
                    paining
               Noticed that during this, lower part of head
               seemed clearer.

               6 mins Pranayama in asana.

               Several days now of a resting on my oars, float-
               ing with the tide, sans emotion, sans desire,
               sans everything. Note a changed mental attitude
               also, possibly best described as objective liv-
               ing, as the purely personal is not troubling me
               these days.
               To some extent, too, I have learned to mind my
               own business.
               All this makes me feel like doing more occult work
               of the mental variety.

7:32-48   Pranayama in Asana.

               HARPOCRATES.
                  Invocation.
9:48-10:10   ASANA.
                  Unsatisfactory, no alertness.
10:10-30   DHARANA, yellow sq & purple egg.
                  Successful in spots. Wretchedly sleepy since
                  nine this evening.

Oct.6
A.M.

        HARPOCRATES. Invocation.
6:17-37 ASANA
6:37-57 DHARANA, yellow sq.& purple egg.
           Neither satisfactory.
         PRANAYAMA, 10 minutes.

         Strange, this feeling of indifference about seeing
         or not seeing the Abbey. I enjoy the social inter-
         course, am refreshed by it, am delighted; but if
         isolated it seems the same.
         (But can this be true deep within me?)

P.M.
12:35   Conscious of top of head.

2:50   Slept two hours, Heavens!

3:00-10 PRANAYAMA in Asana.
           Considerable improvement here over e years ago.
           Three years this month since first seeing Eq'x.

8:47-57 PRANAYAMA in Asana.
         HARPOCRATES, Invocation.
9:50-10:10 ASANA
           Good - alertness in 'aura'.
10:10-30 DHARANA, yellow sq & purple egg.
           Again the feeling that could I concentrate
           more deeply, there would come union - with what?

Oct.7
A.M.
6:20-30 PRANAYAMA in Asana.
         HARPOCRATES, Invocation.
6:40-7:00 ASANA
           Difficult to get into - after that good.
7:00-20 DHARANA, yellow sq & purple egg.
           Good. Last 5 mins vision suddenly went to centre
           of head: interested, so kept it there. Have al-
           ways projected vision before me.

9:39-44 PRANAYAMA in Asana.
           Can do no more. Foot-ball Fives did it.
P.M.
2:55-3:10 Before altar intending to do Harpocrates Silence.
           Having visualized Harpocrates blue, found my-
           self passing over to blue of night. Remained
           here for a time, then conceived myself one
           with Nuit waiting for Hadit - this for a time,
           when I realized some inner something seemed
           opening up. Held for a fraction of time when I
           found myself becoming timid. Tried to continue
           but failed.
         PRANAYAMA, 4 mins.

```
8:47-57      PRANAYAMA in Asana.
             HARPOCRATES, Invocation.
9:12-30      ASANA
             Successful after killing out drowsiness.
9:30-42      DHARANA, yellow sq & purple egg.
             After forming square in front of me took it
             into centre of head. After 10 mins too tired
             to continue. Think there is something to this.
Oct.8
A.M.
6:12-25      PRANAYAMA in Asana.
             HARPOCRATES, Invocation.
6:40-7:00    ASANA
             Feeble
             No Dharana, feeling weary.

             All day at Abbey tending floors.
P.M.
9:38-48      PRANAYAMA in Asana.
             HARPOCRATES, Invocation.
10:00-17     ASANA
             Difficult to enter. After arrival, so strenuous
             had to rest 3 mins before Dharana.
10:20-30     DHARANA, yellow sq & purple egg.
             Most peculiar. When starting, regarded vision
             with what seemed centre of my being, deep, deep
             within; then from just above palate, then from
             womb, then from navel. Ended here, tired.
             Conscious of top of head for a time.
Oct.9
A.M.
6:17-27      PRANAYAMA in Asana.
             HARPOCRATES, Invocation.
6:35-55      ASANA
             A regarding of what might be termed sleepiness,
             but I wonder if it may not be something astral?
             (???)
6:55-7:15    DHARANA, yellow sq & purple egg.
             Again a regarding interiorily.  Will investigate
             this more thoroughly.  This morning do not feel
             beneficial reaction. Heretofore yes - it seemed
             a straightening out of something needing massage.

             Painting of floor of Abbey.
P.M.
8:27-35      PRANAYAMA in Asana.
             HARPOCRATES, Invocation.
8:45-55      ASANA
             Something about me too tired to continue.
             After a rest tried Dharana - unable.
Oct.10
P.M.         Hill for rest.
             Coming from a state of deep rest and repose.
```

'You are soon to reach'---.
Have always thought I lacked curiosity regarding the other side of the door. Am I deceiving myself? If my analysis be correct, I am not.

Oct.11
P.M.

Too tired to do work of any sort. Too tired to paint Abbey floor, but stick at it. Why?
Am I in the inertia of the full stop, the pendulum making ready for the return swing?

At times A.C. amuses, then entertains me. When he is lonesome for his God I love him. Again he bores.

Oct.12
P.M.

All morning I felt whipped, beaten - a great loneliness upon me and desired the arms of a Father where I could weep and be comforted.
I find that in one important particular I have deceived myself.

'Silence is mightier than all thundering'.

Oct.13
A.M.

6:45

Last night I try Dharana and fail: I try Harpocrates and fail. I try lying flat on my back; I accomplish but a trifle.
I then read several Aethyrs and turn in at one o'clock - to be somewhat restless all night.
This morning I again attempt Dharana and struggle for 15 mins - it is a physical pain in my head.
I stop once more and shall try during the day.

9:40

A feeling of change - a going out from this room - something more than a trip to Naples - something thought out by A.C. in Palermo.

Noon.

A.C. back from Palermo and at his suggestion I leave Cefalu this afternoon for Palermo, en route to Naples

Night.

Dinner with Lea at Hotel des Palmes and a talk; she verbally confirms a trait I had assigned to her. Reading of Butterfly Net.

Oct.14
10:30

A very difficult thing for me was the acceptance of Abbey money for a former trip to Palermo - it stung and burned. Yesterday I made a test. I accepted 3,000 lire, having in my pocket a draft for 2100. I feel now I could accept money from whatever source the Gods willed. But, after all, is it a test with a draft in one's pocket? It sounds rather silly.

P.M.
2:00

'Something more than a trip to Naples'.
Poupee? Lea?

(She lay dead)

What a strange look in the face of that child!
Baffling. I have known Poupee in the past, I ^
have known that ever since my arrival and -
if m I read not amiss - I shall know her again!

Do we come in physically where we left off? So I
have been told, but this does not satisfy me:
I must know for myself. And this is where I am
somewhat at sea regarding books at Cefalu.
Since May, 1918 I hunger for, demand, first-
hand knowledge. The music, the vitality of
these books feed me - at times I am conscious
of Force as, in California, for instance, I
could place my hand on the Equinox in Silence
and touch A.A.(I thought). I never felt close
to O.T.O. But the knowledge to be found in these
books must mean infinitely more to some students.

3:00   Without the books, etc., as balance I would become
        lop-sided? (If I am not that already!) In-
        tuition minus science - feminine sans masculine.
        That must be it.

Oct.15
P.M.
7:00   Naples, since 8 this morning. No room until noon,
        so I look up Dr.Widgdorick and then walk slowly
        backm regarding the lay of the city. To my room
        at 12:30, utterly exhausted - the same wearinesxs
        of the past week. I sleep from one until four.
        I still feel like resting so continue reading
        of Butterfly Net, putting down, dozing off, wak-
        ing and reading again. About 6:30 comes an in-
        ternal realization of ~ Purpose? Purpose stripped
        of personality? An elimination of garments that
        restricted. With this comes greater clarity in
        top of head.

Oct.16
P.M.   Dentist, Scala, Rouff, tailor, and a further loca-
        tion of streets, etc.
9:00   Capri.
        I see not the place, it is dark, but I am en-
        chanted! Vision & Voice till I sleep.

Oct.17
P.M.   Naples.
        XXXXXXXXXXXXXXXXXXXXX A bad night
        at Capri, mosquitos and fles, circle entered.
        Also Catholic celebration, bells ringing, monks
        & boys singing through the streets till 2 A.M.
        Slept till 6:30 then up and around the Island to
        see the various grottoes, taking four o'clock
        boat back to Naples, rejoiced to get away!

Oct.18
A.M.
7:22-42 DHARANA, yellow sq & purple egg.

Lacking vitality, but easy. 'Purpose' in top of
head must be linked with lower back of head -
the two to be made one? Will plus Power?

7:45-8:05 HARPOCRATES, Invocation & Silence.
Not yet alive - just words.
Cannot continue.

P.M.
10:15　　　　DHARANA, yellow sq & purple egg.
I find myself utterly unable to do anything.
Have been busy since dinner on Vision and Voice
- not at 14th. (Reading first, with the inten-
tion of going back for study.) Is this the
reason for weariness? I think not - there is
a fag somewhere. Shall try Harpocrates.

Oct. 19
A.M.　　　　A slight entering of circle, similar to Capri.　　?
Used Tao this time and restriction gradually　　'
fell away.
(Time of typing. Think now this was that
caving in of the stomach which I afterwards
recognized as such.)

7:38:45　　HARPOCRATES.
A taking of the Invocation into the Silence to
make the words alive.　　　　　　　　　　　✓

7:38-45　　DHARANA, yellow sq & purple egg.
Could not get hold, then suddenly grasped with
new 'Purpose', which I shall hereafter call
Will, and with that alone (no visualization)
held on. There was a steadiness & smoothness
in holding what was really not there! While
all round seemed rushing waters and fragments
of speech trying to disarm or distract.
After ten mins., tired.

'Pure being is pure nothing; pure wisdom, pure inertia.' 'Pure understanding, silence and stillness and darkness.'

10:30　　　　Walking on the street, I suddenly recall that I
dreamed last night. I confronted a woman of the
Venus type, taller than myself, full figured,
clad in pink silk draperies. I then saw her
back: the robe parted from the waist down and
I saw the parts of a man, gleaming white. Un-
expected, but it did not surprise me.
Do not get anything from this.

P.M.　　　　August, 1918, Fee Wah: I would advise that you
look to your stomach, the blood stream and the
mucuous membranes of the throat' .. 'After all
the love and labour we have bestowed upon you,
you would not dare to fail us through lack of　　✓
physical strength.'

At the time I took such measures as seemed to
me proper, though objecting to drugs took none
of them and tried to effect a cure through exercise, diet, etc.
To-day I go to Dr. Castellone and discover the
stomach contracted inward at the top and the
mucuous membrane trouble spread beyond the
throat into a small portion of the ~~auxiyxxg~~
communicating tissues - to a neglible degree
the doctor says, but nevertheless there and
needing attention and causing some disturbance.
There is still a little uric acid in
the blood but I think this will disappear
with stomach adjustment.

Oct.29
A.M.

Last night, trying, trying to accomplish something
- I know not what - over and over and over
again.

P.M.

At the Museum. My lady in the pink silk draperies: the followers of Dynnisius. But why the
draperies?

I cannot quite get hold of this 'gassy' state.
I am poised and in control, but my mind seems
blown up.

Oct.21
A.M.

Past night I 'sassed' many. They seemed my former
actor associates and always did my bidding
without protest. Always I spoke vehemently,
a feeling I would get my oar in first.

P.M.

Why did I not sooner arrange to take the pictures
to Capri? I am not only detained from returning Friday night as I had planned but must lose
a day, but not being able to get the pictures
from Michaelsen's shop in time to make the
Capri boat. This throws me here till Sunday
night.

And no Hunchback either! I go twice afternoon,
and again evening. Not till after nine do I see
him. Having these extra days I shall now try
to see him again to-morrow, after my return
from Pompeii. Though I need no Hunchback's
assistance to 'make up my mind'. That 'mind'
is under orders of the Will and - Knows!

Oct.22
A.M.

Considerable difficulty in getting to a definite
place - a large, large room and yet it seemed
out-doors - trees. I arrived, moved onto the
floor but later found myself one of an audience

looking on. Mental instruction.

P.M.   Pompeii, Hotel 6:50, too tired to toddle anywhere
             but bed.

Oct.23   Capri, with pictures for exhibition. A cold rain.
             Shivered into hotel at 7, but thoroughly en-
             joyed trip because of a very genial Italian
             whom I encountered going and returning.

Oct.24   Received something definite last night on sex,
             which I cannot explain. I looked at physical
             form, then continued to penetrate layer after
             layer, the skeleton being the spiritual. At
             the end of this experience - for this came
             through understanding, through absorption or
             feeling as I sometimes use the word, nothing
             mental - I traveled up a path which reminded
             me of the Tree of Life, only I went from, say,
             Hod to Tiphereth and, while expecting to con-
             tinue towards Chesed, came back to Netzach.
             There the experience ceased.
         I then left this far field, returned to a nearer
             and clearer one, and joined a Teacher, a man,
             to whom I wished to tell the story,
             but found I could not remember.

11:45   After three or four days of an indescrible stress
             I find myself to-day calm and at peace.
             This evening I leave for Palermo.

Oct.25
P.M.   Cefalu.
             Fifth Aethyr. February, 1918 I saw spheres
             like worlds lying before me, myself on one of
             them. Here I was received by a small number
             of gowned men, wearing stars on their foreheads.
             On entering I bowed low, but was bidden to
             stand erect and a star was placed upon my fore-   ✓
             head.

Oct.28
P.M.
3:00   I try stillness, silence, by uniting of poles as
             I now understand them. Took no note of time.

9:25-35   HARPOCRATES, Invocation.
             Attempting to realize each word.
9:37-57   ASANA.
             Held position and concentrated on complete re-
             laxation of stomach, which has tendency to
             contract in this.
9:57-10:10   DHARANA, yellow sq & purple egg.
             New method keeps me more erect, no tendency to
             incline head forward as heretofore. Visualiza-
             tion about nil but think this will come.

```
                    PRANAYAMA, five mins.
                    Dry throat from cold interferes.
Oct.29
A.M.
7:45-8:05  ASANA
                    A going after stomach.
8:10-30    DHARANA, yel sq & purple egg.
                    Not so distinct, held for 10 mins. Balance of
                    time held Purpose & Power united. Never before
                    have these two been united. This should solve
                    some of my difficulties,- divided city.
                    HARPOCRATES, Invocation.
P.M.
1:45-2:20  Twenty-ninth Aethyr.
2:20-30    Silence in my Temple - waiting.  A coolness as
                    of heights.
                    PRANAYAMA, 5 mins.
                    Nap, 20 mins.
                    Twenty-eighth Aethyr.

                    HARPOCRATES, Invocation.
10:10-20   ASANA.
                    Treatment of stomach, relaxing thoroughly &
                    treatment by breathing.
10:20-40   DHARANA, yel sq & purple egg.
                    Cannot visualize.
Oct.30
A.M.
                    HARPOCRATES, Invocation.
                    Am getting a little more out of this.
7:30-50    DHARANA, yel sq & purple egg.
                    Cannot visualize. Strange when I have no dif-
                    ficulty visualizing afternoons. Held for poise,
                    etc., but something missing.
P.M.
1:35-47    Held, with two flashes of relaxation, myself in
                    Temple, waiting; mind still.  This for past in-
                    carnations.  Preceded by prayer at altar.
                    Twenty-seventh Aethyr.

9:25-40    HARPOCRATES, Invocation.
9:40-10    DHARANA, yel sq & purple egg.
                    Unable to visualize at all. Cold caused coughing.
                    Seven minutes in Temple. Pillar to left, in light,
                    bore hieroglyphs and was banded at intervals by
                    non-cut away stone.
Oct.31
A.M.
6:52-57    PRANAYAMA in asana.
7:00-20    DHARANA
                    I try visualizing - impossible. Then I find my-
                    self looking directly back, all centres of in-
                    telligence awake - this for 10 mins.  Then I
                    look to my left and gradually complete the circle
                    of inspection.
```

If each atom of the body has an intelligence
of its own, why should these atoms not respond
to the Will and do its bidding? Can one see
with the entire body? Hear? Touch? I know there
is something about my entire body, sometimes
closer by, at others far removed from me and
without boundary, that must become conscious,
under control and used by me. What?

P.M.
4:00-40   Prayer at altar.
1:00-40   Silence in Temple, meditation. Strengthening of
          Purpose & Power, an offering of myself as an
          abode of the Most High, a yearning that almost
          amounts to a passion, for union.
1:45   Something now is gone. What has been nigh, nay,
          permeating me?
1:50   I compose myself for a nap. The something returns.
          There is a tremendous assurance - I am in the
          hands of Those who know! I look forward into
          darkness which is yet light and which has a
          quality of vibrant life. And this I seem to see
          with the left side of me?
          Twenty-sixth Aethyr.

9:45-55   HARPOCRATES, Invocation.
9:55-10-10 ASANA   )
10:10:30   DHARANA)
          Nothing. Why is this? I am blocked.
Nov.1
A.M.
7:45   HARPOCRATES, Invocation.
          I am tired mentally. There is a leakage during
          the day? Caused by rigidity or an unnecessary
          grinding out of thoughts?

4:00   A being outside all day, away from any warmth &
          colour. But I have learned to accept this
          quietly. One cannot bring forth all the time -
          the ground must lie fallow, else follows di-
          sease.
          All afternoon I lie quiet, stilling any thought
          as it arises.
Nov.2
A.M.   HARPOCRATES. Invocation.
          PRANAYAMA - 7½ mins.
          ASANA, after stomach.
          DHARANA, 15 mins.
          Impossible, till I found myself regarding sq
          with front of torso - solar plexus?

P.M.   HARPOCRATES.

Nov.3
A.M.   HARPOCRATES.
              PRANAYAMA, 5 mins.
                Jerky, so stopped.

P.M.
12:30   Last evening at the Abbey I place before me a certain Talisman at the request of A.C. I get
nothing. I try again to-day, here in my room.
Get, first, the full face regarding me, then a
body and then something that suggested a tail.
Great vitality in the God. Afterwards I get a
smile, vital, strong. He spkoe but I knew not
what, but I know he has agreed to come again.
I feel a love for him. I ask if I shall take
the Talisman to the Abbey to-night: he indicates
he will come to me here.

1:00   The last shall be first. So I start a sexual record
from the end.
I do not know just when 'John Myers' entered my
circle.
Summer 1908 or 1909 - I believe the latter - I went
to a doctor in New York regarding 'wet dreams'.
At this time and for a considerable period preceding, I had these dreams regularly; i e, once
a month, anywhere from five to eight days after
menstural period when desire was strongest. They
worried me, having heard of sanitariums as the
result. He said there was nothing to do but wed.
But, while I know not when he entered, it was between 1912 and 1915, for it occurred while living in Glendale, California, that, coming one
morning from deep sleep into one of these dreams,
I felt a penis withdrawn - or so it seemed,
though I understood it not.
With the advent of the ouija board and later automatic writing, I discovered who and what 'John
Myers' was, and opened battle. I was about one
year eliminating him physically, i e, after possibly three or four months, rather the latter,
I was in control but there was sensation - in
diminishing degree until all sensation was erad-
icated. Then followed a shorter period of attack on some inner plane, which I do not understand, but which I controlled from the start.
I fancy a year has elapsed since sexual attack of
this character from John Myers'.
All this was brought about, I doubt not, byt the
fact that in my early twenties a man in New York
taught me to masturbate. (I have often wondered
why this was rather than the usual thing?) This
continued for six years, during which time I
fought with my desire to go on the stage - having

been brought up to regard it a vile institution.
However, I finally went to the stage, for sev-
eral reasons, one of them being emancipation,
for I looked to it for sexual freedom.
An Irishman in the fifties took me under his wing.
I should feel grateful - God rest his soul!
Long since dead.
Some time later came Larry, American of Irish descent. He appealed to me sexually on sight.
I really grabbed him. But in a few short weeks
he died of pneumonia.
Seven or eight months later a good Irish Catholic
from Massachusetts interested me sufficiently
to rouse me sexually - being also lonesome for
Larry. I think this was November. We fought
almost from the start because - I could not
tell a lie! I could not, and therefore would
not say: I love you.
The big fight came following March. That was
1910, I remember I was in Florida at the time.
I developed gravel and was in great agony. He
was quite disgusted: 'I thought you were different from other women, but you are like all
the rest, full of aches and pains'. After this
illness was upon me he stayed with me once, I
wanted to see whether he thought only of himself. It snapped the thread, of course, for
unfortunately I could not sympathize with his
becoming inflamed so soon as he saw me, as he
always did.
This was an actor, we were in the same company,
occupying the same hotel. After six or eight
weeks of separation, back in New York my sympa-
thies were enlisted and I consented to see him
once a week. My leaving for California December, 1910 brought this to an end, and left me
with a supreme disgust, which lasted months and
months - more, possibly a couple of years. After
a time, desire returned, but I went my way.
Summer, 1916, a moving picture director, just lately arrived on the Lasky 'lot' piqued me. After
a very entertaining skirmish I discovered him a
University graduate. I was still in the Grades
and loath to leave them. So - exit graduate.
October, 1917 I intended again to take unto myself
a lover, one with a green flag over the 'scutch-
eon. Here one 'Bab' (so called by me for various
reasons), one whom I did not see but who came
first to me on the ouija board and later by automatic writing, entered, explained somewhat of
my past, and told me a lover 'would interfere
with the Plan', etc. I desisted; in fact, took
an oath of celibacy for this life.

May, 1918, when undergoing an ordeal, along these
lines I was told: 'You wallowed in the mire and
dragged down one of great attainment'. And
continued to this effect: You had therefore to ✓
suffer privation - also, You must travel alone
and prove your strength.
But, 'You will spend three years in Japan. Here
your two children will be born'. (A boy and
girl said to have been abandoned by me in a
previous incarnation, so that they starved.)
There were certain other explanations and the oath
of celibacy was absolved.
Therefore, when the proper time shall have arrived, let the Irish beware!

However, these 'two children' are puzzling. On
the face of things and taken in connection with
other statements at various times, I assumed
them to be physical. Nevertheless, I now see a
certain ambiguity, and I am reminded of the
erroneous interpretation I put upon the statement: 'You are to go to strange places in the
emotional world, deal with strange types and
strange people.'

3:30   Again I try the Talisman. I get the God and experience a feeling that I am to be carried
somewhere on the back of a huge something. I
immediately think of huge reptile, with head
of man and with wings, that carried Dante and
his guide, and wonder if I am not confusing
things. I finally go, over upright rocks, the
God apparently not moving but always there. I
come to a cave, a small opening, Gothic shaped,
at the foot of a very tall smooth-faced rock,
rising hundreds of feet upward, also Gothic
shaped. I waver outside, alone, but then enter
and notice the God in front of me, an old man
at a table to my left. Once more I challange,
remembering the diary of C.S.Jones. I then become conscious of intense silvery light, in
shape of a crown, the lower edge partially
crescent shaped. I cannot locate the light. I
look toward the God, the old man, and then
wonder if it may be over my head and therefore
out of my line of vision. Here the vision ends
but with it came a feeling of expansion, of
majesty and greatness.

10:00   HARPOCRATES and Silence at altar.
I cannot concentrate mentally, but find I can
concentrate in that something that surrounds my
physical and that reaches out far beyond it.

This part of me it is that I feel constrained
to work on continually, to build up and strength-
en. Here all petty troubles fall away and I become calm and free from head difficulties. This
thing slips from me at times and then there is
head trouble and the devil to pay generally.

Eve'g   HARPOCRATES.

Nov.4
P.M.   Talisman. Went through a long, round tunnel with
            circular opening at far end - came out into a
            sun-lit garden. Eat fruit here. Passed to left
            over a village lying immediately against a high
            mountainous rock. Was no part of village; noted
            streets in passing. Began ascent of mountain,
            which was dark, damp, slimy. Came out on top &
            discovered I was a huge serpent. Took wings &
            became butterfly of brilliant coloring: flew back
            to garden and lit on outstretched penis of a
            naked body. Think an inhibition entered here,
            for I promptly began to doubt. I said: I will
            start from the beginning once more. Raced
            through from beginning, returned to penis,
            climbed up nude body, caressed neck, travelled
            over face and reached top of head, when rays
            shot upward and out of sight from the head of the
            nude body.
        In this I felt no exhiliration.

Eve'g   HARPOCRATES.

Nov.5
A.M.   HARPOCRATES.

11:30   There is much that I understand now, and I am so
            thankful. There is a feeling of freedom.

2:15   Shummie leaves for Palermo. Hansi shrieks and
            screams at her departure.

3:00   Prayer at altar. I compose myself with Talisman.
            I go directly to my circle of Brethren with
            stars on their foreheads - I rest with them for
            a time, then go straight up and enter a vast
            field of wonderful light, white, soft. Here I
            remain for a time. The light descends - I am
            completely surrounded - from a focal point out
            of my range of vision though I am conscious
            that there is such a point.

Nov.6
A.M.   I could not sleep last night. It seemed to me so
            appalling that a woman, within three weeks of
            confinement, should be sent out alone - to

spend those three weeks alone and to go through
her ordeal alone - that A.C. could have thought
of such a thing! It seemed all the more cruel
in Shummie's case because of her temperament,
which includes so much. Perhaps, too, I was somewhat influenced by the Yi, which said possible
death.

Is it the way of the Tao? 'Unto seventy times seven'.
Also, the matter has brought up a question within
my mind: Suppose an encounter between two, the
one with authority - at least accepted authority,
to send another to an isolated spot, saying, there
you stay without food till you do my will, this
other out of a supreme stubbornness remaining where
sent, the former meantime waiting for compliance,
the latter starving rather than give in. Could a
third step in and feed the starving before it was
too late?

This question has arisen in my mind, presumably because I 'butted' into A.C.'s plan, as I now realize; not deliberately to interfere but because I
did not follow out the complete workings. Please
heaven, with her decision I had naught to do but,
after hat on head, instructions given and she was
ready to leave for Palermo, I said I would send
her money in case A.C. did not do so.

Seeing this in its true light, I shall maintain silence; but from such lack of grasping all details
great occasions may arise. However, it opened my
eyes to myself - may they remain open!

P.M.   A rock climb with A.C., of a variety entirely new
and very interesting. I now realize I never have
climbed rocks.

Nov.7
A.M.   Sleepless last night but I know not why.

P.M.   Very tired all day and I realized during afternoon I
6:30   felt peevish - a simple thing when I am tired.
During afternoon I try work but too fatigued, albeit I get a flaming angel, all in white, when I
use the Talisman and I understand that as I have
dedicated myself to the Most High it is not for me
to seek, but to be entirely receptive, accepting
and reflecting what is given me. Afterwards I enter
a vast, domed, cave-like place, with a polished
floor. Believe hieroglyphs under glass of floor but
cannot see. The ceiling of an uneven texture. I see
a ceremonial chair to left, exceedingly smooth of
surface, brown and empty. I sit in this chair,
regarding vacancy before me and there is a feeling
of repose and power.

This evening the white angel comes again and we go
up a long flight of stairs and I see before me,
high up on a mountain side, a broad, low temple,
white, with Corinthian columns. I enter. The
same sense of breadth and quietness, and here I
rest before the altar and give thanks.

Nov.8
P.M. I work in 'myriad-eyed' body - or is it 'touch'? It
is my will to build and strengthen this body -
every day work is done. In this body lies cause
of stomach weakness? Shall watch this.

Eight mins. Pranayama.

Have had to date four injections of phosphate, for
nerve fag, as I understand. Am feeling very much
better but there is a decided resistance as yet
to resuming the hour's concentration morning &
evening, a resistance which for the present I
shall heed, as I think my intuitions reliable.
Is all the strength needed in the 'body' building?

Nov.9
A.M. A peculiar man last night.
For a considerable time I seemed in magical circles,
going through one experience, rousing sleepily
toss about for a time, then on to another.
In one such I sat in a large hall, rear seat. Conscius
of something going on back of me - turned & saw
various symbols (cut out from wood?) being placed
on wall at height of a man. Star in centre, hieroglyphs on it; four oblong planes placed, two,
horizontally, two perpendicularly, about it,
also hieroglyphed. Then came a blond man, partially bald, not out of thirties, and faced the
star, standing close to it, trying to achieve
something. Presently came the Man, apparently to
help, placing a hand on either shoulder of the blond,
then turning him away from symbols. I saw blond
no more, but noted the Man. Standing by a desk
such as one sees in school rooms, nondescript coloring, tall, with a peculiar way of moistening
lips, and an extraordinarily high forehead. I then
noticed two marks on either side of forehead, high
up: saw they were eyes, narrow, and they looked
as though made of dark mother-of-pearl. The lower
eyes were also narrow though somewhat larger. He
roused in me only curiosity.
Was distracted from this scene by a young man in front
of me who opened a large album-like book and began what he called 'Crowleyism'. I laughed. My
sister now seemed to be to my left. The youth open-

ed a page. I saw a nude woman pictured, with dis-
torted, ill-coloured buttocks; this not confined
to surface; entire mass suggesting rot. The sister
made a laughing remark, easily, without any restraint as I noted, but I do not recall the remark. Indeed, I did not hear it at the time.
We then passed through halls, off which were rooms,
in each of which philosophical or occult studies
were being conducted.

P.M. I feel this afternoon as though I could challenge
all the gods - that I, Jane Wolfe, could dare. ✓

There is a gulf between yielding and bestowing.

I love the God of the Talisman, but he can come or
not. Should he come, well and good; I rejoice.
Should he stay away, it is the same: I rejoice.

Yesterday I saw afar off, to my left but a trifle, a
light. To-day I go after that light, by a path
leading along left side of a high, precipitous,
jagged-edged rocky formation. I find the light is
enclosed in a large room which is a part of the
rock. I enter this through opening like a door-
way but without door, and stand in light, which
is not a flame. The enclosure is flooded. The left
side of base of skull becomes active: a feeling of
expansion. I then rise, straight up, as though
rising on a shaft coming from this spot, and see *in head*
no flames ① a cylinder of fire which I assume to be the sun
and to which I draw near. Then return and remain
on top of mountain peak: here have a feeling of
left lobe of brain being smoothed out - i e, eased.
Focus then passes slowly over to right lobe. I travel
off again and approach what seems to be the moon,
though here I stand farther away than from the sun.
Meantime the right lobe undergoing some experience.
Again return to rock, unite two lobes, and now realize
one as light, the other as darkness. Then followed what impressed me as first glimmering of 'oppo-
sites', the lobes being double-barrelled, the
'sight' back of them.
Interrupted here by Giovanni's "Signora! Signora!!"
If I do not answer, he thumps on my door, and when
I do answer he gets mad because I do not understand!

Nov. 10
P.M. I fuss around all day and do nothing.
A.C. off for Palermo to meet Russell.

Nov. 11
3:30 I use the Talisman, feeling drawn to it. The God puts
a.m. me on his left shoulder and we rise into space -
up and up. Then I see below me, slightly to my

P.M. left, a rock projecting, the earth lying far, far
below - I see this earth to the right. A nest
of eggs - three. The words: Fecundate them. I
wait a moment, then 'How?' A tiny black serpent
appears in the nest. Again I wait - then, 'Now
what?' From one, to the left slightly less than
45 degrees - i e, emerging from the egg in that
direction, stepped a white bird: I see its feath-
ers distinctly - about the size of a pouter pig-
eon. This bird becomes a white pillar, which rises
& rises up, far away into the sky. I watch -
nothing else happens. I then return to the nest -
having gone up with the pillar - and from the egg
to the right there flows an inky fluid; it spills
over that side of the mountain, continuing to flow.
'What of the third?', the centre one. This is a
wee, wee white bird, that perches on the edge of
the mt.shaft, not far from the nest, and sings
happily.
The sky between the pillar and the inky stream now
fills with x huge head and shoulders of a man; the
thing dark and apparently chagrined..

I am reminded that from 2 to 2:40 I sit in silence,
waiting. During this interval a limitless sea of
blue, myself in the centre and something strong &
moving received through the palms of my hands when
in contact with the water. I cannot analyze it
without getting into the double. Do not attempt
this as I understand I would then leave the physical.

All day the desert has called - I ache for it.   ✓

11:30 I sleep a bit and wake. I get A.C. saddened greatly,
and as though I were the cause. I walk by his
side, steadily, up a stony trail, gaze ahead. Just
so he, too, walks. But this something proves a
bond.

12:05   . . . . . I pray you hold
Me as a secret and a blessed chrism
That you have gained to adorn your house of gold /
By some strange silent sacred exorcism.

Recollection: Before falling asleep, I saw standing
before ma rocks; facing me, a colossal figure,
hoary headed, flowing beard, with trident in the
right hand. Neptune?

Nov.12
P.M.   All day I type record - also attempt to clean paint
from court. No lye, no water to rinse after scrubbing. At 2:45 try occult work, but nothing definite

except I stand by the vault of light, high up on
the rock of November 9 and A.C., clad in red, comes
up the steps. I can get nothing regarding his
mood or reason for being there.

Later. My being swells out and floods the universe! One I
love has been with me!
       Hold me as a secret and a blessed chrism.
So do I hold thee, O beloved, who hast the wide
heavens in which to spread thy wings!

Nov.13
P.M.   At 12:30 I lie down to rest ~ cannot sleep. Rise,
1:15   go to altar for prayer, then work. The flaming
              angel takes me by the hand but I can get no far-
              ther - some confusion. I then banish any and all
              vision and hold silence, letting nothing enter.
              There has been a force of some kind against me,
              like a wind, in which I could not compose myself -
              this for some little time. Now use Tao and finally
              become one with that wind. Then realize all emo-
              tions of the world are a part of me - that all
              breath is my breath. From this I pass through top
              of head and spread out like a blanket, covering
              many, but I cannot make these many a part of the
              blanket.
              Then I find myself back with flaming angel, who takes
              me by the hand, raises me to his level - the spot
              to which he has descended, and I discover myself
              in a white robe, a narrow filet about my head. It
              seems like a confirmation and I stand, as a maiden,
              before the threshold of life. Am conscious of a
              name ending 'iel' - Auriel? Aniel? Iliel? Amiel?
              Unable to grasp fully and think A.C. will know.

2:35   Does 2 mean anything to me? Yesterday, just before
              beginning work, two sounds, one on table, one on
              case of drawers. Tarday Just now, while my head
              rested on altar, came two faint but distinct ticks
              on wand lying there.
              (At present do not like phenomena.)

6:00   A.C. back from Palermo without Russell, which I re-
              gret. How he must get bored with naught but three
              women!
              He says: Lea has told me much about you. It might
              be interesting to hear the 'much', having discov-
              ered my first week here her incapacity (as I
              thought) to report conversations correctly, but
              having come to the conclusion - after the fanciful
              story of the California pal - that she falsifies
              deliberately.

10:00   Such an element of doubt - it all seems rubbish! The
              truth is, I suppose, I am equally bored.

I say: "I am content - I have patience", but it is a
lie. My slowed-up mental (?) reactions are humiliating at times.

Does one who likes to be lied <u>to</u> want his vanity
tickled?

Nov 14
A.M.
11:50

Supposing yesterday was "confirmation day", I have made
a wonderful start. Here I sit, possibly moody, pos-
sibly peevish; opaque; dull, reflecting nothing.
And perhaps not trying to rouse myself. I accused
Bickie of taking a voluptuous enjoyment in moods
- a sexual debauch. Heavens! ???
I feel as though turned loose to pasture , to see what
I would do. I challenged all the gods. Now it is
up, maybe, to Jane Wolfe.
I laugh, for I see the humour of the situation.

Shall one do violence to one's self, thinking thereby
to please or entertain another?

Seeking justification for acts - a mental or moral
screw loose?   (Slave spirit" 3rd tea)

12:45

I feel I could freely relinquish all.
Thus let me live, unseen, unknown,
Thus, unlamented, let me die;
Steal from the world, and not a stone
    To tell where I lie.
Is this laziness?

For people's achievement I care not, though all the
world be at their feet. But what they suffer -
then can I achingly yearn!

1:22

The impression of going a different way from that
planned. One not quite so clear - more inscrutable
- more difficult?

1:40

I enter the silence; I cross a threshold, a large arch-
ed gateway. Before me lies limitless smoky mist -
I see nothing, but directly at my feet begins the
descent.
Clear eye, open mind, no thought of self to cause
fear, confusion, or faltering.

Shaddai puts me in temple, there is a peal of bells,
the most ornate Chancel I have ever seen - indescribable in its richness, forms and color of ornamenta-
tion. A.C. stands at distant altar clad in white,
the red robe beneath shimmering through. He faces
me with plate on which is broken bread. I do not
get close to the altar, nor do I eat. Confusion
here.

Find myself adopting watch words - Open mind. No thought of self.

Nov. 15

A.M. Have noticed for a short time a sense of well-being mornings, as of reserve strength. Wonderful! Satisfying, gratifying.

An indescribable renunciation had to be made in regard to the vision work that I cannot grasp. Yet I definitely, consciously renounced.

I have in the past sought the Elysian fields of bliss - thought I was all wrong unless I roamed there. Wrong.

Live, not know.
I so infrequently in the past used the physical medium; got to the point where I knew I was a city divided. Made a point of bringing myself back, again and again, and shall eventually develop a sound mind in a sound body. Now know the beneficial effects on the physical of so living.

Obscure

Prayer?

P.M. Silence and prayer.

2:00 I enter the grotto with the large brown chair. A huge dragon-like monster which rears up, his head touching top of dome and drawn back against throat as does a spirited horse at times, the body arching backward and down to where I see two legs similar to those of a crocodile. His back over these two hind legs is distinct, hide of crocodile but there is a horny ridge in center, the tail long and trailing into darkness. I cannot visualize details of body. It snorts through large bulging nostrils. Nothing repulsive, nothing slimy - great strength and power, and a sense of green somewhere. I climb onto back over two hind legs. I shoot down the tail, way off, come to a circle of red, gaze at this puzzled; then grasp away blue, which now encircled red centre, race back over dragon, up its back and to head. (What happened to the blue?) I remain suspended in space trying to visualize completely the face. While doing so, feel love for this thing permeating me. It immediately prostrates itself, rests happily at my feet; and I feel it is now a helper, servant, to do my bidding - glad to do it.

Shadow ✓

On a high mountain, in a room of a homely house, a man seated by a table with a book, lamp to his right. I face him. He rises, goes to a shelf to his left, takes from it a book, which he places before me, open. Something there, but I cannot read. A large tome, parchment covered. I depart with the book,

see it carried by my double in front of me, a purple
silk marker flowing from it. I descend the mountain,
attempt to read, pages appear blank. Turn to frontis-
piece - can see no picture, but in lower left-hand
corner I see blue and know there is gold above it.
Opposite is printing, and I understand thexbxxk my
name is there. Get nothing more: I wait.
The book fades away in smoke, and I see horses' stamp-
ing feet, I foõlow up the legs and the picture is filled with mounted horsemen, carrying spears and banners.
In the centre, more visible than the rest, a youthful
figure, suggesting a Jeanne d'Arc or Christ.

9:30   For the first Harpocrates has meant more than a silence
by stilling. At the altar my heart overflowed toward
Shaddai and to him I poured my oblation. I then went
on to Harpocrates. Came a partial vision - a field of
white light with a something in the centre I assumed
to be Harpocrates, while below stood Shaddai - he
quite distinct.

Nov. 16
12:20   Impelled to altar. Here got impression "sin", vicious-
ness are servants - to be commanded.

1:45   Attempt work: wish to learn about book. Amidst confusion find myself back in room from which I got the
book. See smaller one suspended between me and book-
case. Cannot decide between the larger one with me
and the smaller one, whose cover suggests bitterness.
(Christian conscience? The first was given me, therefore I should look no further. Why did I go back?)
Impelled to altar. Impressed while there that alcohol
fumes from my brain feed something in a pitch-dark
cave, where waters lap greasily. Can see nothing but
know that slimy things are in that water.

(I took one glass and a quarter of wine, and am quite
conscious of of the fact.)

2:50   Myself seated, as a colossal person - almost an image
- feminine but dominant note, power. This for a time.
Then appears circular enclosure, Egyptian, open to
the sky; tiled floor, alternating black and white
(white, greyish with age?), with large red circle in
the centre, point of each tile pointed outwards. To
my left a large stone lion, resting on a base almost
as high as a man.
To my left and in the rear, farther away, a doorwayd
into a room, high-ceilinged, white. After a time a
very, very small figure, in black robe, suggesting
A.C. Stands in doorway.

10:00   Did I get too close to the slimy things in the greasy
water? All afternoon and evening am in a "mood".

Went into Fives in this mood, scrapped; continued,
and through Pentagram, and it is still on me.
I, and I only, can cure these things.

Nov. 17
A.M.
11:00   Am very tired - in the emotional body, the focus seeming to be just inside the back in the region of the
diaphragm.
Or, I wonder, may it be a spiritual depression? Grey
and monotonous, like the day.
Whatever it be, it is not through the head.

Nov. 18
A.M.   Restless during night - some bit of magic. Waked about
mid-night, silence, and sensed a great breadth,
calmness and stability of - what?
Late morning dreamed I was packing trunks to go away,
being married. Groom there, but did not see his
face. All very matter of fact. Going to a lake
district with mountains and tall green trees all
about. Groom hung rug that was in my possession,
though not belonging to me, so as to keep in good
condition till our return.

P.M.   I get into same breadth and stillness of last night
and remain poised here a long time, eradicating
that which has distressed me for two days.

Go off to left and descend onto round knoll of earth
- I see the granules of earth plainly, reddish-brown,
and see a small circular opening, shaped like a
crater, this centre filled with something white,
Shaddai   suggesting the whiteness of fungus growth below
earth's surface. I regard this (it is level with
the earth), then dig around it, try to pull it out.
There is no change whatever. I move away and regard
it, then ask: Is it a penis? The white spot elon-
gates into a penis, white, about the height of an
asparagus shoot. Nothing else happens, though a
white angel has appeared and stands quietly, with
a broad bladed sword in left hand, point resting on
the earth.

Here, feeling the need of rest, as I have not slept
well for several nights, composed myself for a nap.
Dozed off a moment, then became conscious of inward
desire to write. Then came directly toward me, the
body streaming horizontally through the heavens directly away from me, a colossal Being, white of soft
whitness; a strong sense of whirling mightily yet
was he stationary. Our two foreheads touched, I
trying to pierce through his. He then seemed to become to become a large pillar in front of me and
slightly to the left, my entire body resting against
it when first visualized. I then stood back, regard-

ing the two, for the Being was there once more, the pillar now a solid mass like granite with a wreath around its base, which was square. I then turned to the left, walked past pillar, low coping of same material and colour, and came to an arbour, low, covered with grape vines through which the sun streamed. Back of this a small, white, plastered house, one story. I waited. Noticed space between house and fence to left. Walked round house and saw entire space back of it, enclosed with a fence and a large gxrdxnx piece of land, was an arbour covered with vines through which the sun streamed. Back quite a distance, on the left side, sat A.C. in the brown knicker suit with a book on his knee. I walked down the path which lay in the middle of this garden, and stepped across the unpathed portion lying between him and me. Here there was some confusion, for he seemed to stand, again he remained seated reading Rabelais. But he surely was stand, though the vision was dimmed considerably and myself almost asleep, when to my right, a short distance back of A.C. near the fence, was a goat with long grey hair. Roused myself, looked back toward the house, and saw an old-fashioned bake-oven, which had been white-washed but the face of which was smoked, from the opening, upward. It had a roof sloping backwards, this roof supported by poles at the four corners; no side wall.

Later.   Once more I touch foreheads with the Being and shoot straight up, receptive for something to descend. The Being soars up toward me and I start away with him. I then notice betrayal - it is not the Being. I go back to the sky but the spell is broken. Then return to true Being, get strength and return - higher than before, and seem flattened against the sky to receive something. It seems like something I shall write.

Nov. 19
P.M.   Prayer at altar.

30' Silence. First I seemed to concentrate in a something quite extended above my head, the body steadying and furnishing support, this something like a baby taking its first steps. Then followed what seemed a turning back of mind(?) upon itself, a closing up into complete stillness, and I had the feeling of waiting on an outer rim while the inner, the solid or circle, was still, without motion. A deeper stillness, I think, than ever before experienced.

3:45   Shaddai. Up stairs hewn out of rock ¯ entire stairway hewn out of solid rock. A landing, steps continuing upward. Door to left, pushed it open, entered¯ Dark-

ness. Finally became conscious of something in corner of room, to my left, red some place with this
"something". Thought, a man - it was a snarling
beast. I passed it, and entered another passage-
way, level, lighted by lattice window. Saw ahead
a lofty spacious room, entered; empty: passed on
to wide verandah, built high over a vineyard, the
ocean beyond.
The place wonderfully pleasing, happy and calm.

Nov.20
P.M.   Prayer at altar.

2:00   On closing eyes immediately became conscious of bril-
          liant white light, far off; and I did not see this
          light as I have seen other visions. It seemed at
          the other end of the "wire", and there was great
          happiness and rejoicing. At this end I reflected
          somewhat of that Love. Then I became conscious of
          colours, a mosaic it seemed, and tones correspond-
          ing to those colours. Afterwards these colours be-
          came a mass of flowers which fell by me, and out of
          the sky trouped myriads of people, but there was
          not the brilliance of the first light.
          I was tired when starting.

          Kept silent for a time, then realized I was seeing
          with an entirely new set of eyes - part o that
          "subtle body" on which I have been working recently?
          Former visions impressed upon upper fore-part of
          head. This part now still, while something about
          lower part of face and shoulders looked at pyramid
          shaped rocks rising out of darkness, the apex no
          lighter than of an evening.

          Read a bit from "Moonstone". Put it away, with an
          automatic "Thank you", as though somewhat was done
          for me and start work.

3:15   I regard again with "subtle body", this time from chest
          and stomach region, and see a garden walk leading
          down to a gate in a stone and cement wall. I see
          apply trees - no, in shape between an apple and an
          olive - I see bits of grey moss on their trunks. A
          hill rises back of this. I sense a water trough to
          my right and slightly back of me Then find myself
          looking from centre of my back and see the home, of
          stone, I think, with posts supporting balcony. There
          shade trees all around, they seem like sycamores,
          the bark is white flecked. To my left the ground
          slopes downward and this is an orchard.
          ① back of water trough, with roadway between, a
          shed for vehicles, space for three, I see no horses.

          A wonderfully peaceful, homey scene, the entire scene
          in nature's colors, most realistic I have yet seen.

As an experiment use forehead.

Two horses, first bay, second black, in darkness on
    left-hand side of shed, in lean-to, feeding from a
    manger, their rumps toward me. The private road-
    way leads over slight rise between path and shed,
    a pile of loose stones next to lean-to, a cherry
    tree growing beside it, the path to gate dropping
    lower and lower from roadway and at a slight curv-
    angle to left.

Nov.21
1:20   Prayer at altar - ears ringing as of high-pitched metal.
P.M.

Spheres floating about.

Russell arrives

9:30   While sitting in silence after Pentagram a happiness
        permeated the centre of my being - a something def-
        inite, it seemed, though I understand it not.

Nov.24
P.M.   During night a voice, as though my own, arguing for a
        "dream" - time and again - but there was no re-
        sponse. Strange this should come up again after so
        many months.
    However, there is pressure along the line somewhere.
        During my first weeks at Cefalu I suffered agonies
        through the top of my head - incessant chatter and
        great physical pain, that caused hysterical spells.
    Again is something upon me - since Nov.14, so subtle I
        did not at first recognize it, cumulative in effect.
        Noticed closely yesterday and now feel confirmed.
        But this is (it seems) inside the centre of my body.
    I could regard it as pressure to look away from self,
        for stopping to regard this, and therefore in a way
        feeling somewhat of it, I cannot hold on - I feel
        shaken toward insanity.

Attempt silence - nothing doing.

Nov.25
P.M.   Prayer at altar.

1:40)   Silence - 20' with new Talisman at foot of bed, mo re-
2:30)   sult; 10' placed on my foot, no result.
        Silence without Talisman balance of time.

9:00   An enfolding peace and deep, in the centre of my being.

9:20   Just finished my work at altar.
        Shaddai talisman I took to my forehead - many times
        have I touched it so.
        New talisman I take to my breast. What is it?

This is all worry; why this Emotional strain? You are to look at a talisman as a botanist to look at a new flower (You placed Shew-Stone on forehead) J.W.

Nov.26
A.M.

Dreamed a woman made sexual love to me - i e, kissing
my lips - yet she did not kiss them. No impression
made on me. Hardened sinner.

Shummie's baby born at 2 a.m.

P.M.
4:00

Talisman. Visualized symbol above head, steadily -
shaft of yellow shone down on top of head

Heavens! A new emotion. I ached to use my riding
crop over a bare face - to inflict fearful pain.

9:25

? Is it possible?

Celebrated Lulu's birthday. A.C. gross at table. Evening at Abbey bored me horribly. They speak a language I do not understand. Shall I ever understand?
And the drugs? Jones, says Russell, is fond of
aether. I do not understand that, either. Think I
will experiment to find out something here.

Nov.27
P.M.

Silence - part of time beneath a tree with heavy fol-
iage. Afterwards saw large rocks in desert - not
sharp or peaked.

Every day, at some time, I become hysterical - this
for almost a week. Something must happen, for I
cannot sleep. Either this thing spills out of me
or I collapse. The singing of birds is so much
noise. I cannot work, I do nothing.

Nov.29
P.M.

A smooth day! Take a short dip in the ocean.

2:00

Prayer at altar.

Tired, so compose self for rest. Instead take 30'
silence, then rest. Not exactly, for something peculiar is on my mind. Then come steady rythmical
taps of specific number on my bed, but I cannot follow. There are 2s, 5s, 3s, and once I counted these
to 11. Went to altar and tried for number there,
but no response.

7:00

A.C. reads Liber B during Pentagram.

Harpocrates at altar.
10'   Dharana, yel sq & purple egg
       No visualization - held vacant spot.
       Held sq above head, with subtle body, with forehead.
8'   Dharana, yel sq.
       Got sq, but poorly.
       Pranayama, 10'

Started memorizing Book of Law.

Nov. 29
A.M.   Slept better last night than for weeks, with a further
          elimination of "preference".

20'   Dharana. yél sq.
            Visualized only after giving yel sq a green back-
            ground, placing back of me for some time, then in
            front for legs to look at.
            What is this "subtle" body into every part of which
            must be born sight?
          Pranayama, 11'
          Harpocrates, 12' - Poor.

P.M.
2:19   Prayer at altar.

          20' Silence. I am definitely off visions at present,
            it seems.

          With each elimination, a drawing nearer to "under-
            standing in the world" - that which I must achieve.

          Memorizing Book of Law.

9:00   For 30' I attempt visualization, silence; and can do
            nothing - my head will hurt. Shall memorize Book
            of Law for a time.

Nov. 30
P.M.   Prayer at altar.

          30' Silence. Russell thinks, from my description,
            this "subtle" body is the astral.

          Memorizing Book of Law.

          5' Pranayama - wobbly breath.

9:00   Tried Silence, could not.
          Book of Law.
          Taps on bed, one - one, two; one - one, two.

Dec. 1
A.M.   Between 10 and 12:30 last night, witnessed rites in
            which A.C. and Russell took part, it seemed -
            not really definite. Came in into physical conscious-
            ness with strong odour of goat. Thought: "How can
            my sheet smell of goat?" When fully awake, no
            odour, of course.

          10' Silence. A breath restriction with silence this a.m.
          10' Pranayama.
          12' Harpocrates.

P.M.   Prayer at altar.

2:00   20' Silence. Offering self, a receptacle for use by
             God.
         15' Silence. A heap of sand on desert.
          8' Pranayama.

         ¼Capsule of grass.

8:55   Since mention of analyzing thought, have been wonder-
             ing why, during some part of the past, I was al-
             ways on the defensive, belligerently eyeing all.

         Harpocrates at altar.

         Attempt yellow square - it continually recedes and
             disappears.
         Silence 5' - pink and yellow wands, like huge candles,
             three of each.
         After lying down, a most radiant blue breaking through,
             something like daubs or splotches.

Dec.2
A.M.   10' Dharana; yellow sq. Feeble.
         10' Silence.
             I cannot breathe, restriction.

         Affiliation oath, at Abbey.

P.M.   Leave for Palermo. Wait 3½ hrs at station, then go
             to hotel and stop with Shummie - a dreadful dinner.

Dec.3
A.M.   A most ghastly night - possibly 2 hrs sleep. Take train
             at 5:30; arrive 7:40. No money - sit around for
             bank to open.

Dec.5   Cefalu.

Dec.6
A.M.   20' Asana.
         20' Dharana, yel sq
             Placed sq directly back of me.
         Harpocrates invocation. Attempt silence.

P.M.   Prayer at altar.
         20' focussing and energizing astral (?).
         Memorizing Book of Law.
         4' Pranayama - wobbly.

         For the first since my advent in Cefalu feel an inter-
             est in my work. Heretofore mechanical only, which I
             do not understand.

9:00   20½ Prayer at altar.

20' Asana.
18' Dharana, yel sq.
    Held directly beneath my feet - good for 10',
    then short conversation bet.Shummie &Russell
    distracted, and could not again recover.
15' Harpocrates.
    Invocation in silence.
    Good - stillness of mind.

Dec.7
A.M.   Wakeful all night - read 3 hrs from Woman in White
    without soothing. Cannot concentrate this A.M.
    Dull headache, stomach bad; mulled wine and
    some irritation the cause.

P.M.
2:30   Am still in mood where I care neither for goods nor
    men - where I could shut the door in the face
    of any - where I feel this whole business was
    not my choosing but was thrust upon me, willy
    nilly.

I know the feeling well

10:00   20' Asana.
    Steady, no movement.
20' Dharana, yel sq.
    First 10' good - regarding sq.with my right side.
    Disturbed by Russell coming in; floundered
    around for 5', then recovered somewhat.
10' Harpocrates.

Dec.8
A.M.   After last night's work, composed myself for sleep.
    Colour on an orange tone - this from centre of
    myself, as though I were a circle, the colour
    appearing in the centre of that circle. Then
    landscapes - the first I do not remember. The
    second a long, low-lying range of hills, with-
    out trees, the sea back of them a deep, deep
    blue, the hills reddish; there was yellow some-
    where in the foreground.
(Why did I not write this last night?)

20' Dharana, yel sq.
    Regarded square with left side. Great difficul-
    ty in pinning down mind all through.
15' Harpocrates.
    Intense and still, body glowing with warmth.

P.M.
2:15   I have been thinking my work was to sit under a Bo
    tree and wait for the universe to pass before
    me. Of course, "Wait for God" means just this
    thing from one angle, for the universe is God.
    I prepare the vehicle by all means possible,
    train the horse for the Rider. I the trans-
    mitter of the electric current, the step-down.

Quibbling serves one purpose, at least.   Serenity
or lack of it, depending on "moods".   The "fric-
tionless" way.

15' Close work on astral.
6' Pranayama.

Memorizing Book of Law.

3:50   ½ Capsule of grass.

8:30   My affections are not offended (therefore do I love?)
but my prejudices (?).   Is this egotism?   I see
no vanity in myself.

A bomb thrower.   These are always feared and distrust-
ed.   The shepherd comes along, over the ploughed
ground, feeds the sheep; and he is loved.

Drugs to free centres sooner - i e, open up: at this
time to hasten the Aeon.

Lea asked: "What does I N R I mean?"   Russell makes a
reply, which I have forgotten.   I say: "You may
recall seeing it in Catholic churches; pictures of
Christ on the cross."   She answers: "O, yes", and
nothing more is said.
Did the mind stop working - there is a tendency to
accept that with which one has grown up, or has become familiar with through association.

Various methods of initiation - some by way of sex.

20' Asana.
Good - a something new infused into this - a taking hold--by all muscles of body?
18' Dharana, yel sq.
First 10' good, seeming an eternity. Last 8 a
struggle to hold on. Physical same as Asana above.
17' Harpocrates.
A struggle to do this at all. Tired from above.

Dec.9
A.M.   20' Asana, good.
20' Dharana, yel sq.
Poor - nervousness in stomach.
Think now stomach due to a fear so subtle I cannot
yet dig deep enough to unearth. Had thought it
due to suppressed emotion.
10' Harpocrates.
Nothing but words of Invocation.

Tired all over after this work.

P.M.   Rejoicing at altar.

         12' Work on astral, taking each side of body in turn,
             then left and right of head, then uniting all
             into one. This work steadies mind.

         Book of Law.

         10' Silence.

3:50   Capsule of grass.

10:00   No effect from grass, though I have taken ¼ additional
             capsule. Cannot work, so read Adonis.
             Has the cold aught to do with this?

Dec. 10
A.M.   20' Asana, strenuous.
         18' Dharana, yel sq.
             Regarded entirely from what seemed cerebellum.
             This left mind free to wander while the rest of
             me was still and focussed. Noted this, though
             held mind quiet for most part.
         10' Harpocrates.
             Tired after the above.

P.M.   40' Talisman. With Shaddai talisman sat quietly, vis-
             ions forming fluently through front part of head.
             Here entire astral (that on which I have been
             working for some time) regarded. Felt drawn
             away from earth (?) - something left far below,
             fading away entirely, I suspended in space. So I
             remained for 25', I think. Sensed black, though
             saw it not. Then noticed black serpent, long &
             thick, with yellow mouth and eyes. A feeling I
             was on a planet in the heavens.
             (When first sitting with this talisman, got a
              black figure among rocks.)

10:00   Capsule and a half (at 6:30 the ¼), no result except
             to incapacitate me for work. Albeit cold may
             be responsible.

         Finished reading Adonis.

Dec. 11
A.M.   Cold still with me - awake much of the night, and up.
             Astral in bad condition this a.m. because of my
             emotions. No work. Feel weak too from an intes-
             tinal disorder.

P.M.   Prayer at altar. Talisman.

2:30   Past 15' trying to get control of astral - no.

Talisman. Put myself in square, low-ceilinged room, underground, in darkness; and tried to pierce that darkness. After a time became aware of brilliant eyes, sharply regarding me. Tried to see body - shrouded in darkness though I sensed shining ebony. Broke away here and found myself in very long, spacious room, with floor of black marble, with pink roses. Do not know how this room was lighted. After a time, books along entire left side of room and I became conscious of infusion into myself of rosepink. I accepted the black of the floor but the pink roused my curiosity. Then noticed green was combined with pink in tessalted floor. An exceedingly rich, cool interior.

10:00   ½ Capsule of grass at 3, ½ at 3:50. Drank wine, 2 glasses to help along. Only effect was light headedness, the forgetting of sentences as A.C. spoke them (though I do remember the gist of the conversation-- History Lection, publication of rituals, etc., as I had drafted business letter to L.V.), and the seeing his face change into many different faces, some of which I knew.

Dec.12
A.M.   20' Asana, vigorous.
    20' Dharana - on astral, rather, no yel sq.
    12' Harpocrates.

This way of working must be that of A.C., automatically unfolding. It takes more strength, more concentration and makes me very warm all over. This way the body may, in time, become automatically rigid, as I understand that phrase.

Letter to L.V.Jefferson re agency for sale of books, etc.

P.M.   Capsule of grass.

2:30   Visualizing self constantly - mind constantly making unformed pictures, resulting in "Bwouze", so the word sounds as I hear it - a bwouzed line, for instance being a line with mossy-like fragments, a something floating away from the line, which should be distinct and clean-cut.

Visualizing and speaking at same time. Half-formed pictures; speaking symbolized by organ pipes, each beat bringing pipe higher in the picture. All bwouzed.
(Would be glad if someone can tell me what this means)

Not bad

Left lobe of brain feels as though there were a gimlet hole clean through it - I can look through the it. (Am conscious at times of just this spot.)

Experienced an affectionate regard for something. This regard, flowing out, was like unto a calf gambolling about - I mean the same rythm, a certain crudeness for affections.

Dark movement on desert.

Valley with stream,   outlined by green - there was white along water's edge.

A black spot, which later became a globe. From this an Altar arose; a flame, I heard "Shin". Then this disappeared, and a very luminous red-gold Sun, low on the horizon, blazed over altar. Picture ended with outer ring of illumination from sun touching outer rim of black sphere, the altar being no higher than this black rim.

Figures, suggesting mounted Arabs, all white, flowing by.

Seemed to break through something of myself, and expanding beyond this particular body in which I have been.

Outside, looked downward on head; in crown a round opening with blood along edges, congealed, also flowing down. Saw no hair.

Found head hurting here. Took hold and stopped it. Then entered a home which had key-note "safety". Looked through large plate-glass window, showing beautiful garden, rocks and water beyond. House modern. The entire picture giving a semi-circular impression.

Where are thoughts? I see a dome, chambers all round the circle supporting dome, the centre hollow up to dome. This dome blue (cannot read rest of notes)

Desert, then took shape pinnacled castle, flanked on either side by hillsides. Brilliant outstanding, which when first beheld before seeing castle, suggested arm outstretched with beaconing light, like Statue of Liberty. When at castle noticed the light was on the top of an iron rod above the castle.

Dec. 13
A.M.   Awake long before daylight - no more sleep.

20' Asana.
   Strength gone when finished.
   Yesterday noticed force pass up spine, flow into
   head and strengthen. This a.m. also.
   (Then why tire? Jan 2)

Another scrap at Fives. This the kind of scrap that
   I enjoy - it fires me and makes me play better.

P.M.
2:00   Capsule of grass.

3:00   Is this loveless thing my true self? If so, why was
   I chosen for a work that requires all love? Is the
   mind loveless? Yes. What is the subconscious?

No

Love left me when I drew out of the station at California. Montana was hell. New York was a comparison with the ten years before. Mr first trip
   across the ocean was, just the trip across. Some
   things amused, many bored. The friends in Paris
   were fresh water when I was thirsty. I dashed
   through to Algiers and on to Bou-Saada. There I
   knew happiness, rolled up in a nice comfortable
   rug, as it were. On going to Bou-Saada I squabbl-
   ed about Arabs sitting beside me in the coupe.
   Leaving there I wanted them by me, I loved them.
   But, again I left love behind me.
   Have I known it since?

If you know

What part of me is it so rude and crude ⁻ indeed,
   insolent at times?

4:00   Two flashes of Love came through, invigorating mind
   and body, causing me to be sympathetic to all?
   What is this that tells me I have loved.

Was Wilkie Collins in love with Marian, but afraid
   of her. Not the kind of woman most men love -
   rather is that type the friend of women.

Became a part of L.V's mind, understand it better
   than ever before. Think I will have to get
   A.C.'s mind from the top, down.

Mind is - should be, a fine, clean instrument.
   Sensed what seemed spirit trying to look through.
   The two lobes of brain united ascend and become
   slender woman in blue, with high head-piece suggesting something Egyptian ⁻ cannot get correct
   design.

Saw a light far, far off. Rose toward it, tried to
   reach and become it, but could not.

Tried another way of rising - up over a high mountain.
   Past trees, over shrubbery. Started from a well.
   Came from vast height back into body and into spine.

It is the Divine must love.

Animal soul to be loved and respected and made a part
   of Divine.

Expansion of centre back of eyes.

8- 10   Reading Psychology of Hashish.

Lights out!

Dec.14
A.M.   Waked about 3:30; no sleep. Read Diana of Inlet.
           Turned in at 6:15. Waked at 8.
P.M.
8:15   Tried work this a.m. for ½ hr.but cannot recall re-
           sults. (Why not make entries at the time, any way?)

This noon could not work on scenarios - thought to
   type record, muscles sore. Tired, tried to sleep.
   Could not. Tried to work at 3, could not.
So let everything slide·

Now I feel in a humble mood, ready to take my place
   at the foot of the class - where I belong.
   What have I been doing, what attaining since
   May, 1918?

Steadfastness.
   That which will prepare me for the Work.

Took first grass Dec.8, end of second day responded
   as to gentle laxative. Disorder grew, increasingly, rising to a crescendo, leaving me weak. No
   grass to-day - this evening bowels quiet.

Dec.15
A.M.   Good night's sleep - no indication of intestinal
           trouble.

20' Asana, good.
30' Dharana, yel.sq·
       Good, in spots. Picture of clean machine given
       in grass vision of 13th excellent help. This
       should eventually eliminate the "bwouze".
13' Harpocrates.
       Got this by focussing on the lotus. What does
       this lotus mean?

A bit of the outer fuzziness is being eliminated.
The degree of concentration is better in all this
work. This applies to the last few exercises before taking grass.

P.M.
2:00   Try concentration - impossible. A cigarette made my
whole body shaky.

Book of Law. To end now of Book I.

Work on - what? Left side of me, for 20'. Could not
continue because of Lulu crying. Usually this does
not disturb me.

10:00   A little work on Tree of Life.
20' Asana.
Unable to do any other concentration, so reviewed
Book I, Book of Law.

Dec. 16
A.M.   Rather light sleep, for I was waked frequently.
5:50 started Asana, 15'. Rested 10'
Started Dharana but worked instead on astral.
Rested 10'.
20' Harpocrates.

This strenuous work on astral is bearing fruit. I
feel more set up, psychologically? The negative,
lassitude, is fading away. I am better able to
look away from self.

Letter from Hansen regarding Equinox - $1500 in all.

P.M.
3:00   Notice I respond more readily to stimulants. My
Naples medicine intoxicates. Also I feel a cig-
a rette. The medicine must be doing its work -
the dry throat which occasionally waked me gasping
for breath, has disappeared. So that long-standing
catarrhal condition is on the mend.

8:35
8:55   Rejoicing before my altar. My being poured itself
forth in thanksgiving; I could not find the words
and used Psalms. Then, too, I got my first rythmic
movements for dance - not definite enough for memory, but a beginning!

Dec. 17
A.M.   Busy all night but, alas, I cannot remember. A.C.
was there, or his influence overshadowed.

I cannot work, but feel in no way disturbed. There is
a general relaxation.

P.M.
9:30   Could not work all day - a good reason.
(Wish I knew, Jan.2)

Think I must be after the chakras. Waded around for
several minutes, finding every travelled road
blocked. Then felt consciousness travel down body
to hip section. Worked from left to right, completely round body, then took sex centre and worked
definitely on that. 20' in all.

Dec. 18
A.M.

35' Asana on astral.
During night mind felt tight, "chatter" floated
across it. Recited Book of Law, but with drowsiness and lack of control when falling asleep mind
would again start up. This morning drove something
out of - heart centre; the centre of the physical
body.
Other work on upper part of body and head.

There is a certain splendid something about Lea, something fine. Again a spiritual communion, but a
spot in me is contemptuous of her. What, and why?

10' Harpocrates. Entire consciousness focussed in -
astral?

This form of concentration - in astral? - is the most
strenuous I have done, but there is a feeling of
well-being afterwards; a physical fitness results,
as did not the former way. I notice it during the
day, also - perhaps more so.

P.M.

Prayer at altar - became conscious of stone while
at altar.

2:30

A pillar composed of many stones - it stood to my
right, I directly by it. (Heretofore everything
has been to my left) On a slight elevation. Water
flowed from base of pillar, in front of me, clear.
Started off from left, at an angle; did not will
this, consciously at any rate. Went far, far off;
accomplishing nothing, I willed myself back. Then
appeared before me, xxdxfxxingxxx, a figure of masculine appearance, raiment soft white, diapanous,
dark hair. Could not see face. I challenged this
figure; it neither answered nor departed. I said
nothing, nor did I approach. Figure then left me,
descended hill, joined female waiting there and,
arms about one another, departed. Then, to my left,
was impressed by a feminine attribute of this male
figure xxd that it needed me.

3:00

Then came one, in the same place, who seemed black,
but I noticed on close inspection the robe was a
black-violet. This one faced me.

Do not understand either.

Your complexes
resent her
simplicity, which
is her one & only
asset
not it is to be found in
her subtug purtugration for
new acts in any toy her
farnesis. I. W,

6:15   ½ Capsule of grass.

10:00   Worked on a scenario - Cached Ruby - do not like it
          at all.
         Afterwards tried work - grass!

         So began analyzing.

         Dignity seems to be completely around one- The sense of

         Sense of steadfastness from along spine.
         Sense of looking away from self just above the ears.

         There is a feeling in me of proud assurance.

         A beautiful blue, when closing eyes and concentrating.

         Faith of child, without convictions, realizing child
          ignorance.

         I cuddle and protect something that needs up-rooting.
          What?

         Something lazy.

         Astral sediment.

Dec.19
A.M.   No work - there is an inner fatigue.

         Reading in afternoon "Comment on Book of Law".

Dec.20
P.M.   Finished reading of Comment.

         Surprised about construction placed on Scarlet Woman.
          Like the idea of Hierophant and Priestess - BUT

         Three-fold Book of Law, three-fold Thelema, three or-
          deals in one, thrice-armed, etc. May there not be
          three here, also? Hierophant and Priestess; Beast
          and Scarlet Woman, she as unique and designated an
          individual as he and not by him to be deposed (as
          I assume to be the case with Priestess), and a third
          deeper meaning?
        For: In her "is all power given". This suggests to
         me the powers of a Christ.
         "She shall achieve Hadit". Did any of the six so
         achieve? No! Else would they not have failed.
         Then how can they be the Scarlet Woman?

         (If my vision of Jan.11,1919 had to do with Lea -
         as I have been told - why Bertha Bruce at a later
         period?)

Please dismiss this

I din't understand
all this myself

Verse 53 ". . ; ever To me! To me!"

Verse 62 " — To me! To me!"

Verse 65 "To me! To me!"

I know nothing of Qabalah, but what of this?

"The child of thy bowels, he shall behold them."
Who shall say who does know these mysteries - who
is capable to judge if Jones be the "child"?

P.M.
9:15

Palermo. Villa Igeia; no room at the Palmes. Full of
freaks here. Men with queer noses, receding foreheads, eccentric slouches; women all colours of the
rainbow, blue-lidded, red-lipped, bobbing ear-rings,
protruding shoulder blades, mincing gait, loose-
lipped and tight-lipped. Each and every one extremely self-conscious. A continual pose. Each eyeing each, a measuring of swords. Very entertaining.

Shummie does not go to Naples, one reason a "plot" -
at least those words were used to me. Why fear?

Live your life so you can look every damn man in the
face and tell him to go to hell.

Dec.21
P.M.

Shopping all day - nothing interesting.

Is economic freedom the first step towards sex free-
doom? Of course; booby!

Dec.22
P.M.

Finished work in Palermo. Took Siren and Desolation
to Daneu's for exhibition and sale. Returned Cefalu afternoon. After dinner took two small doses
morphia. Smoked opium evening; left Abbey at 11:30.
Vomitted before retiring.

Dec.23
P.M.

Sick in morning early; did little all day; read a
scenario or two.
After dinner two small doses morphine. Smoked in
A.C.'s room, bunked with Russell. No definite visions, but felt there was but a thin veil between
the conscious and subconscious.

Dec.24
P.M.

In Abbey all night - felt good on arising; short nap
in afternoon.

A little typing, read Duel Deferred and Noble Nobody
- Fives - some mail.

Opium record.

6:00 - 3 pills)
6:30 - 3 ") Sensed leaping flame; did not see it.

6:44, ditto.
  Thought: "The Capsule", scenario - crooked for the
  sake of villany. Why not for a reason? x

7:00 ditto

7:30 "
  A quick flash of something suggesting star-strewn sky.

7:45 ditto

8:15 "

8:30 "
  Saw poetry - verses of four and six lines - occa-
  sionally a single line.
  A large hand holding a pill.

8:45 ditto

8:55 Head of a youth, lying on left side of face,
  round eyes turned upward, regarding me. Very still.

9:10 Pool covered with lily pads. Near me a round,
  flattish terra-cotta coloured bowl, highly polished, empty, bowl about 15' diameter, 3' high.
  To left, though not connected with it, a tripod.
  Made of iron, slender legs.

9:25 A black beetle, small of body, legs of some length
  - moved sidewise, travelling downward directly
  in front of me. Red some place about its head.
  This incoherence of description due to having
  fallen asleep before taking in all details.

9:30 Too sleepy - something with small stones - almost
  pebbles.

10:00 Called on Fee Wah for assistance in ascertaining
  mystic name for myself. Wrote his symbol three
  times, then visualized same, then called.

  On elevation similar to terrace in front of Abbey; a fine, beautiful foot-way of stone, cement
  and carefully-formed coping, leading downward to
  a small city lying, whitish, at the foot of the
  hill. Over the whole scene, which included palm
  trees, asoft yet brilliant sunshine, very clear.
    To my left a low-lying building, into which

x There are
"reasons" for
everything, of
course; but the

average man
is a crook; so
why emphasise
explanation?

I intended going, when I realized Shummie was to my right, slightly in the rear. I did not see her - I just knew she was there. Her unspoken thought that the trip down to the town would be very hard for her physically, turned me away from the door, and I started toward the foot-path. I felt she had womb trouble.

This faded, and I heard twice "Mathonet" - "Mathonit"? Then I argued: "No, not 'Math', but Manothet.

(A.C.'s interpretation follows.

Manotith or Matonith = 516 410 + 106 = 516
   = The female Fish
Thom = 65
ON = Nu 56
TMAT = 50 Jonah's whale
   = female Fish
   = Gates of Binah

Maton = 106 = Nun
Mat` = 50 Gates of Binah - (Adamah ▼ of Chesed,
            watery earth - Jonah's whale
            the Sea Athm = closed, shut up.
On = Nu   Thoma = unclean
Ith = feminine termination.
~~Manotith~~, Matonith is the Lady of the Hidden Understanding of Nuith.

Now 516 = 6 X 86 The (Sun) manifestation in radiant harmony of the Female Elements of Nature, brooded upon and impregnated by the Breath of h the Holy Spirit, or of Nuith, whose letter is He.

516 = The radiant manifestation of Nature, inspired by the Breath or Holy Spirit of Our Lady Nuith.
516 is the abstract idea of this.
Matonith, the concrete correspondence, the Woman who incarnates this idea.)

Dec.25
P.M.

Waked up rather ill - bad headache and general lassitude. Slept in Abbey. Went to Umbilicus and to bed till 11:30. Somewhat refreshed.

I must learn, somehow, to bring things through. This evening a very illuminative couplet regarding "Filth", so called; that phase of life in a nutshell. I understood all. When this finite mind grasps that in a moment, clearly and definitely,

will it constitute an "illumination"? Is it in
this way that Illuminations take root?

Dec.26
A.M.
A dream. And a dream that amuses me in spots.
A large house. In one room, upstairs, my mother in
bed, a man seated by the bed. She was young and
did not resemble my mother as of to-day, yet she
was my mother. She told me I would find a certain
something in a certain room, do not know what; it
was to be obtained by me because I was leaving the
house. I went to that room, and in it I found a
young woman in bed with a baby (woman resembled
Mabel Normand). Some one else in the room, to my
right, near a window. If I got anything I do not
recall it now.
Preceding this I had been accepting the amorous em-
braces and ardent kisses of a man in a hallway. We
stood by a doorway. He endeavored to break down
what stood between us. I enjoyed all this.
At some time I noticed I was clothed in a close-
fitting, rich, heavy silk gown of a deep hue; mul-
berry, I think, or the deep violet shades of a can-
yon. I also wondered why one, say ten or twelve
years younger than myself should be so desirous
of me.
After leaving the last room, we met once more in the
vestibule, where I gave a lingering hand-clasp,
kissed his hand, and said: "I wish I were not a
coward", and departed. As I left and crossed the
street, I thought how theatrical my farewell, how
insincere my words, for, from the start, I knew it
was not my will.

11:30
All morning the personality of this man, whom I can
not recognize, has clung about me, I cannot shake
it off. Rather slender of build, slightly taller
and dark.

P.M.
7:00
Typing, Fives, a little reading.

I ask Russell for a Tarot divination of my dream.
Giovanni, this morning, brought a photograph of
Jones. I receive a certain shock: the photograph
suggests the man, but I cannot be sure.
   Russell says he does not believe there is any
connection between Jones and myself - the cards
also say no. He further adds that he thinks there
is a connection between himself and me. And proves
it by the Tarot.

Reading in Equinox.

Dec.27
A.M.
Could not work last evening because of gas pressure
in abdomen. Stomach bad for two days. So lay down,

*always the
attraction
between old &
young.*

meaning to work so. Nerves of lower legs extremely
sensitive, and jumping. Went to sleep, of course.
Waked up during night, and tossed from side to side
a long time; chief seat of difficulty nerve ganglia
from nape of neck downward the length of a hand.
Why should this be when stomach is, apparently,
the cause?

Peculiar dream about A.C., my mother and Lea - my
mother, of course, making it so; and this time as
she is to-day. Lea and A.C. in bed, my mother lying on the floor. I thought she had in some way
deceived me, and I at first resented the lie. Afterwards was able to eliminate my prejudice, whatever it was.

Bad headache.

Attempt Asana and Dharana. 40' sitting still.
22' A ka dua. Difficulty all the way - stumbling.
Found when, on a few occasions, mantra ran easily,
a part of me could think of something else. Like a
Catholic counting his beads and watching everybody
in the church.
8' Silence. Good. Broke here and could not again
get back.

Dec.28
A.M.

Yesterday asked Russell about unpublished Equinox.
He thinks it fine - rough on Christianity - great
magical opposition. And as to the publication
thereof: All eternity, a million years (or some
such statement), the gods are not worrying.
But -
While all eternity is at our disposal, has not
A.C. this incarnation, and this only, in which to
get all this Aeon work started?
Do we incarnate to accomplish a certain, definite
work, and therefore does not time enter in?

Took 3 small doese of heroin last evening. No result
so far as visions are concerned. Eyes affected, as
with liquor - slightly. Vomitted crossing the hill.
Deep, restful slumber.

Waked this A.M. 7:20 - try work but cannot accomplish
anything. Have not done any of my concentration
work nearly as well since experimenting with drugs,
but there can be no loss as I feel some complexes
have been eliminated. Due to drugs, or had the
time arrived for elimination? Why has liquor not
done this same thing?

P.M.

Russell to Palermo on 5:35 a.m. and back again at 8.

Why do I continue to be so upset? Feel as rigid
physically (and therefore mentally) as a rusty engine. My stomach bad, bad.

I see the portrait A.C. painted last night - in about
half an hour! Incredible and beautiful. Also did
he give me a small panel, which satisfies me but
which he says is not a picture.

Dec.29
A.M.   Still all awry physically. Try work - cannot. Repeat
Book of Law, Part I - stumble on fourth page.
Nothing in my room to read. Must keep an Equinox
on my shelf, for occasions - or a Bible.

P.M.   Try work for almost hour, but cannot.

Late.   Pentagram - A.C. explains Creed.
In exploring River of Soul does one take account of
material existence only? If so, why? If life one,
individual, why not continue "between the acts"?

[handwritten margin note: Lea asked one same question! answer: because there is nothing to record; it is the lives that modify one.]

Light seems to be gone from me. Must watch these
periods closely - they have happened before - and
see if aught takes place before, during and after.
However, come to think of it, love flowed from me
for two days past, which surprised me. Not to-day.
In fact, felt peevish, but that was stomach. Improvement here, I think.

When shall I be out of this trackless waste? And
what is it that is cut off? "We shall take your
intellect". Can it be that? I feel at times I
have no mind, only will to keep me going. But
what works, and that so lamely most of the time?
There must be no depression, therein would lie
danger; but I do get very tired and sometimes long
for freedom.

Dec.31
P.M.   Still upset.
Got ready for mailing The Apple and The Capsule,
and enclosed in letter to M.K.W.

[handwritten margin note: ?]

Had one lucid moment on couch after Pentagram and
felt fine. Looking over "Test Course", was getting,
I think, something about printing press for Abbey
when A.C. interrupted about the Simon Iff stories
for screen.
(Query: Had "Indo-American Press Co." aught to do
with this?)

Leaving Abbey, muscles of legs ached by the time I
reached the mill - faint and nauseated when by the
brook. Wretched.

(P.S. A.C. says foregoing due to carbonic gas from charcoal)

11:00   Just preceding unconsciousness of sleep, mind repeated distinctly "3-16-21"

1921 Jan.1
P.M.   Feel somewhat better. Played a game of Fives - typed on record.

Jan.2
P.M.   Same report. Typed on record - Fives - a colorless day. Would like to have an active two weeks in a totally different climate.

Naturally! But there is a time to stick things through; apoptosis - going blossoms to Osiris. And sooner or later one has to do this, or one never becomes master of one's environment.

1921   Jan 3   Wakeful night; repeated Book of Law, Part I.

Try work; cannot. Everything makes top of head
     hurt; conflict of some sort.

P.M.
7:38   ½ Capsule morphia.

8:15   Three pipes opium

Classical atmosphere ; tradition beautiful. Would
like complete realization of this - I think I
mean more knowledge along these lines.

8:45   3 pipes
9:20   3 "
9:45   A shiny vase on a square, velvet-covered base.

10:25   3 pipes.
A Mongol face, black hair of unusual lustre, a
sword, broad blade diagonally across face; ¼ circle of white around.

Are visions of the mind only?
Well ordered mind producing better than ill-ordered
     one? *Yes*

Jan 4
A.M.   In Abbey all night- nothing; about 3 hours sleep.

Re responsibility. A.C.: "Lea says you shirk responsibility." True, and with malice aforethought.
I may be right, I may be all wrong in this. Time
will have to tell. *It will*

P.M.
1:20   One thing the matter with me: Am not appreciating
opportunities. There is still proud defiance -
defiance of god and man. When I could be withered
at a glance!

An opium evening - nothing.
Slight naßeau.

Jan.5
A.M.   Sound sleep, and restful.

Some mending for A.C.

Work on "Sooner or Later".

Opium, beginning at 7:15
About 9:10 heard voice like a child's: "Yes, me
too - - - all foggy".

9:37 EOEON (heard)

Away from this physical body, but too incoherent to
remember - was not sufficiently controlled - what
I got was fragmentary and quickly forgotten. Heard
voices as in ordinary life.

Toward morning vomited.

Jan.6
P.M.   Capsule of morphia.

7:20   3 pipes
7:40   "
8:00   "
8:20
        Dreamed of eating radishes.
        A part of a rite said frequently, Lea in unison.
9:30   3 pipes
        A being in another body, in which everything was
            perfect; i.e., I could see the perfection of all.
            Could not bring realization through.

Jan.7
A.M.   Dec.31 I made entry about printing press for Abbey,
        but did not enter all, challenging my reading at
        that time "India-American Printing Co". I seemed
        to receive the impression that Comment on Book of
        Law would be printed on press of Abbey, but could
        not follow this up because of the aforesaid inter-
        ruption.

        Have read on "Paris Working" these last two nights.
        Finished this morning and have better understanding.

P.M.   Read Liber Thirty-One.

        Opium - no morphia.
        No results.

Jan.8
P.M.   ½ Capsule of morphia.
        Opium during the evening.
        In places where movement is very slow - my body
        moving slowly.
        About mid-night. Tell Shummie somebody will be fat
        and is to be called Matalon - or was it Matalone?
        (Did not get who the somebody was)

Jan.9
P.M.   ½ Capsule morphia.
        Opium.
        "West 92"   "Madison Avenue, Mrs.Webber, 492".

Jan. 10   One week opium - no appreciable results. Restful
            sleep - being waked from sleep not disturbing -
            constipated, but appetite the same.

            During this period I noticed that whenever I waked
            the earlier part of the night, the muscles of
            the pit of the stomach - or was it the region
            immediately below the stomach? - were taut, con-
            tracted. There was a definite holding on.

            To-day the noises of life disturb; they jar. Pres-
            sure on ear-drums. Also, for a short time, the
            feeling of no moorings.

Jan. 11
P.M.   How one's heart bleeds for one who really suffers!
            And I can do naught but stand aloof, silent!

Jan. 12
A.M.   Stomach dreadful. Last night that same nervous
            state in upper arm that I noticed last time in
            legs (Dec.27) Opium before.

Jan. 13
P.M.   "Sodomy artistic". In what does art consist? The
            scrubbing of a floor may be made as artistic as
            the painting of a picture - hoeing corn the most
            divine poetry. Does art lie in the soul of the
            artist or in the act done? To the Philistine
            copulation can be just as artistic and pure as
            sodomy - also can the latter be a debauch.
            There must be more than that back of it.

Jan. 15
A.M.   Body asleep, on another plane cam vision of land-
            scape - small lake in foreground, then brown
            house, back of it forest of green trees. This
            I hastily shut off. Why? Not consciously, at
            least, have I said "Not it". And there was
            nothing repellant or fearful.

            Have discovered some thoughts, like cripples,
            staggering along, haltingly and with step broken.

            On another plane (body asleep) found myself walk-
            ing around a white unoccupied bed, in a large
            room suggesting a hospital, as though expecting
            one I knew to occupy it, ill.

Jan. 16
P.M.   Why when I would speak are my lips so dumb! I
            wish to express my supreme interest, my deep
            concern - no words come: only gesture rises in

me. On other planes I have speech - why not on
this?

Date unrecorded.
A dream. Absent from Abbey, though I know not where.
Returning found a woman present, of a nervous vital-
ity, shall I say? Magnetic? She held my attention.
Knew A.C. in America. After a time a man, also
known by A.C. in America, seemed to be of the party.
These two then went away together.
(man + woman)

Date unrecorded.
Opium.

"Resist not evil" - life through friction. Indif-
ference the deadly sin and deadly means. Things die
when not nourished by love, interest or hate.

Entered large banqueting hall - empty. Table set
up en regle. Heard scrap of conversation between
goblet and other table accessories.

A page, a youth differently garbed from aught I have
ever seen pictured, bowed low and presented me with
a package of typewritten sheets, the first page of
which was entirely in symbol.

Entered oblong room from another oblong room, at
right angles to it. Room entered, large, built of
logs, plastered between and whitewashed. A sense of
light and cleanliness. Large oblong table stood in
centre of room, woman seated, back to me, at left
corner of table nearest me. My sister seated to
right between table & window, my mother standing
farther up the room in line with sister. Neither
had a head. I soliliquized: They move about, are
alive, work; therefore they have heads though I see
them not. Then I noticed pale blue about my mother.
In upper right-hand corner, set diagonally across
it, a large wardrobe, door of which was plate-glass
mirror.
The three women sewing on most elaborate silken
gowns.

At another time during night and in another place,
the same working on elaborate wardrobe for Lea.

Jan.27
P.M.   Article on "Contemporary Portraits" has again sent
me on the track of "live for expression only". It
matters not what others think or do, what they are

1921

or who they are. This world is the little red school-house,
each one here for its particular lesson, its particular experience. All that is necessary is to bloom -
whether in well-kept garden, by windy roadside, in
depth of lofty forest, on arid desert plain, or
alone on mountain peak. What is it Whitman says:
I give to men of my store. If they accept, well and
good. If they reject, it is equally good. I pass
along rejoicing.

Should I feel sad though all reject my food? They
may have just as good - or better. And though it
were worse, still what odds?

This leaves one free from striving, free from am-
bition, free from "yearning to serve", itself an
albatross. One energetically blooms, pouring out
one's soul for the joy of pouring.

Am seeing beauty in Cefalu!

Jan.28
A.M.   A.C. off for Paris - Lea as far as Palermo with him.

P.M.   For the second time in Pentagram felt that Russell
was once a son of mine.

Opium, but it does not please me.

Ah, the red pipe! Strong, like that of a longshore-
man. I mend the silver one with adhesive plaster.
There is a bouquet, a pleasure in the smoking.
No results.

Jan.29
A.M.   The life of the Abbey, its inmates, have not in all
these months entered my dreams, excepting A.C., he
possibly three or four times. Now, suddenly, I
dream.
Lea and the dressmaking orgy.
A.C. and Lea (two or three nights before his departure), they at that time coming in for a most
furious onslaught by me, over a "book to be returned to the Astor Library"
(Lea told me something 2 days before leaving)
Last night I dream the Abbey in celebration of
Lea's third pregnancy.

Opium - no results.

Jan.39
A.M.   Keep the good work up!
Dreamed A.C. and Lea in what impressed me as a sexual debauch, on the floor at my feet. I noted and
then left the room.

Jan.31
A.M. 1:30 Went to sleep about 10. During this period have
been going through what seems ceremonies, rituals,
studies, or what? A.C., or his influence. (I
suppose I mean by "influence" that which he has
ordered done, or which, by some means, he is able
to do himself without being visible at the time.)

7:30   This is becoming amusing!
On a knoll, park-like: many people, divertisement,
etc., etc. A king - the king desires me. I become aware of this almost immediately and try to
elude him. Slip through devious paths, down the
hill, across a street on which, if I remember correctly, ran car tracks, and reach a large lobby.
Here I ask clerk back of desk to announce me to
a definite man upstairs, a man between whom and
myself was some understanding. The clerk delays,
eyeing me lazily. I implore, as I know the King
and two, I think, assistants are following. Clerk
lazes toward telephone just as King, et al, enter.
They take me to a large room upstairs in which
are three beds, the first inside the door to left
very wide and uneven, the next one beyond with
two farthest legs broken or off, as that bed tipped toward the window, a third at right angles opposite the foot of the other two. On this we
sat. Facing the door was entrance into another
room, where I saw two French bedsteads, in excellent condition and well dressed. Their colour
was pink that had a bit of purple thrown in.
A woman prepared me in some way I do not remember, then she and one attendant left. The second
remained and I saw him removing his shoes.
The King then kissed me, but it was not with
lips. I would liken it to a serpent's tongue
playing on my lips and chin. I thoroughly im-
passive.
Then found myself in a different room, talking
casually with second attendant, he very dark-eyed.

Feb.1
A.M.   Half-past three yesterday 1 capsule of grass, one
hour later, ½ capsule. Enormous appetite at five,
which I indulged with Mortadello, glass of wine
and liquer. Hit bull's eye with Shummie each
time I tried. Genesthai's witticisms missed fire
with her. Returned to Abbey to get fire going
for Pentagram. Sat in kitchen waiting for Turkish
coffee, and three times essayed what G. said was
"rising on the planes". This so new I noted only
sensation of going, expansion, and wondering if
I could remain a unit or fly into a million frag-

ments, and could I ever again get myself small
enough to enter the physical. Is it safe to try
this now? I feel like experimenting.

After Pentagram stomach discharged superfluous food,
as all good stomachs should do. Thank you! Felt
very good.

During evening lay on couch, Shummie beside me, her
head resting on my elbow the better to read. An
impression of two boys, 3 or 4 and 7 or 8, dressed
in rich velvets, I the older, a self-constituted
buffer, shock-absorber and comforter of the younger
- we virtually prisoners inside spacious walls. A
feeling of isolation and loneliness.

Being the first of February, shall begin my schedule.

7:15-35	Asana, a sitting still. Feel last night somewhat.
7:35-50	Harpocrates.
	Fair; broke after 10', again in 5'; then force gone. Last 5' better than first 10'.
P.M.	Worked on two geomantic figures, one for Beast and Paris trip, one for self for next two months.
9:17-35	Asana.
	Mind wandered round geomantic fig. & other things forgotten.
9:35-53	Dharana, yel sq.
	Made comparisons with Dharana work heretofore. Think I have discovered a leak.
	Tried Harpocrates, but failed.

Have noticed how much better Russell does the
Pentagram since departure of A.C. and Lea. The
feeling of restraint is gone, there is force and
much better reading.

Feb. 2
A.M.

7:35-55	Asana.
	Mind wandered considerably.
7:55-8:10	Harpocrates.
	Difficulty until toward end, when I seemed to catch something new.
P.M.	
5:45	All afternoon on 12 houses of geomantic fig.
8:33-51	Asana.
	Mind wandered at first every where, but afterwards pinned down somewhat. A clear, dispassionate instrument only!

8:55-9:10 Dharana, yel sq.
        Well nigh impossible at first. Sq seemed thrust
        down neck, lower ends invisible. Finally got it
        in place. Broke after 10' for a moment.
9:15-25 Harpocrates. Nothing.

Feb. 3
A.M.   No work - headache.

P.M.   During day a little typing, a little work, a day
        in which there is no life in me.

8:30-45 Asana. Good.
8:50-9:05 Dharana, yel sq.
        I cannot understand this lack of ability to
        visualize in this exercise! Used to get these
        squares, and squares with purple egg.
0:10-30 Harpocrates.
        Break after 10' - finished; an improvement on
        Dharana.

Tried vision work afternoon and evening without
success.

5' Pranayama.

Feb. 4
A.M.   Wakeful, so tried visions.
3:00   Not successful with B U E R
        Used:
        "Thee I invoke, abiding one", etc.
        Repeated over and over, going through space, first
        four lines. After a time came to a gold rock.
        Hazy impression of small beings with bodies and
        heads especially round, thin legs. Passed by them,
        and over some distance, noting this place was off
        in space. Nothing more.

        Called on Mak Melchizedek (because of his connec-
        tion with the name Matonith). Came to a large
        door, of most excellent perfection, finished in
        white and gold. Lines like those on cover of Konx
        om Pax, though at different angles, the white
        bands, some up, some down, being outlined in gold.
        Did not get through - at least this was all.

P.M.   Lea back from Palermo. No work, as we talked
        over much.

9:35-53 Asana, cross-legged on box in East before altar.
        Excellent.

9:55-10:15 Dharana.
                Have floundered on this ever since resuming
                exercises. Battled again, ~~then discovered~~
                then discovered that mind stilled, the "inner"
                held receptive - waiting for God, attitude of
                attention to receive - seems the thing for
                me rather than sq. Became still to all sound,
                pain of ankles on box, etc.

                This Asana and Dharana best ever experienced
                for concentration. Feeling of strength and
                repose when finished.

                Harpocrates, 7'.

                Some thoughts in Asana - Dharana any thought too
                weak to register.
                Genesthai regarding schedule.
                Where pot was placed in room.
                Suppose fouly diseased body desired A.C. and
                Lea (Just read Abbey record & their oaths to
                give body to all who desired)
                Just who was Semiramis.
                Two or three others during last 10' - these
                during first 10'.

                Bed at mid-night.

Feb.5
A.M.
7:30   15' sitting! No Asana at all - heard every tick
                of watch, every spade thrust of peasants.
                Found myself straining, so quit, hoping to
                work later.

10:30   Still confusion - Giovanni moving trunks, etc.

P.M.
9:20   Asana. (All work now done cross-legged in East)
                Not so concentrated as last night. Lea lying
                on couch, moving slightly at times, discon-
                certing. Good practise, however.
9:45-10   Receptive. First 10' fair, last 5' weak.
                Pranayama, 8'

Feb.6
A.M.   Early part of night ceremony of some sort.
                A hearse the focal point? Horsemen and car-
                riages arranged in large open space. The
                Kaiser seemed a part of this.
                Ceremony began by man on horse - a mistake made.
                Immediately second rider did something which
                balanced it and therefore nullified error.
                A white horse here but do not remember whether
                first or second.

7:20-38	Asana (in own room)
7:40-8:00	Harpocrates.
8:00-15	Dharana.
	All fair for morning.

Silence began this A.M.
Umbilicus family arrived, each saying the familiar line. I stood cudgelling my brain; finally remembered something, said it, with the
remark: "Well, I got that out of my system,
Genesthai"!

11:00	Pranayama, 5' Wobbly.

Have felt shaky all morning - "on edge". Why?

A different personality seems looking out of
Lea these days. Too, one evening she looked
strikingly like my brother, and for the first
time I have seen a resemblance to myself.

P.M.	
3:30-4:00	Try visions - unsuccessful.

Then sat myself on a rock out in Space, to rest.
After a time became conscious of green-grotto
green, like soft clouds beneath me, then pur-
ples and violets, while some deeper part of
me sensed a white brilliance far off and beings in that brilliance.

8:35-55	Asana.
	Fair, broke twice.
9:00-15	Dharana
	Broke after 10'.
9:15-25	Harpocrates.
	Tired, I think.

Feb. 7	
A.M.	Waked 3 A.M. to control "dream" - did so.

Slept till peasants waked me 6:45; continued
aleep till 7:45. Much refreshed.

10:00-20	Asana, in East.

Equilibrated self in large temple (?) shaped
Restful. Thoughts about physical hunger,
took in purple curtain at altar once. A waiting for God.

10:25-43   Dharana.
        Used "Thou who art I". Result excellent for
        equilibration. Broke 10:37

10:45-11:00 Harpocrates.

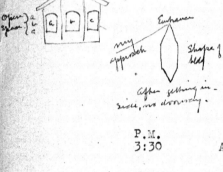

        Difficult. Later climbed a very high moun-
        tain, no trees, no rock, a carpet of wiry green-
        black moss, with greyish edges. A look-out on
        top, a small white building with rod in cen-
        tre top. Entered. Tried silence - nothing.
        Looked through open space: First seemed to
        be above everything, only space, then to my
        left and some distance away, another pillar-
        like rock. Did not see its top.
          Then noticed bldg. had 6 sides, each side h
        the same length but placed so as to make bldg.
        oblong.

P.M.
3:30   Assembled correspondences of Capricornus on
        typewritten sheet to facilitate work.

4:00   I make a discovery - at least to-day I was un-
        able to turn round in a vision.
        Inv. "Thou who art I"

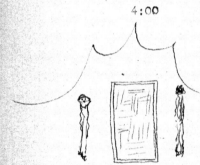

        "Melchizedek" door, white and gold, with an angel
        on either side. Am not sure of top of door-
        way but think it has three points. Went in-
        side, got confused. Returned, and began
        studying exterior. While deep in this passed
        to vast interior, all white and gold, and
        pillared as far as I could see. Passed along
        line of pillars until I came to what seemed
        a central part. To my left I thought I saw
        a seated figure. I wished to stand in open
        centre, turn to right angles from present
        position so as to have full view of figure, &
        found I could not turn to my left. After
        fruitless effort thought to pass along, but
        there was nothing else.

        So, I get some visions after all. Thought my-
        self definitely off for the present.

        10' Pranayama - another improvement. 10-20

9:20-40   Asana, in East.
        Difficult in spots - mind would consider self;
        the three years following May, etc.
9:40-9:58   Dharana.
        Not satisfactory.

10:05-25   Harpocrates.
           Extreme simplicity in spots.

Feb.8
A.M.   As I would rather do Yoga before the altar, I
           have put French in the waking hour - Yoga after
           Fives and while Lea is in Cefalu, 10-11

7:30-8:00   French.

10:10-30   Asana
10:30-45   Dharana.
           For both, get and lose; when "got" good con-
           trol. In Dharana "waited" before Gold disk.
           Equilibration good.
10:47-11;07 Harpocrates.
           Interrupted after 5' - not satisfactory.

P.M.   Typed letter to Bickers & Sons, re Chiswick stock.

           Little work on Capricornus correspondences.

3:03-14   Pranayama - somewhere lost a minute by cough.

3:40   Well, the Baron has gone! And I have my little
           joke with Lea - "All who may desire me".

7:30-9:00   113, 161, 284, 2911

9:07-25   Asana, in East.
9:27-47   Dharana.
           Much difficulty for 5', then seemed to take
           hold with centre in throat.
9:50-10:10   Harpocrates.
           At no time, a battle to stick it out.
           15' Pranayama.

Feb.9
A.M.   Slept throughout the night! Heretofore waking
           about 3. Physical being seems tired.

7:30-8:00   French.

9:45-10:05   Asana.
           Frictionless. Thoughts, but cannot remember
           them when finished.
10:05-25   Dharana.
           Got into this when taking hold with centre
           in throat. Steady.

10:30-53   Harpocrates.
        First 12' good. Then removed coat, as an ex-
        periment. It did break up things. Feeling
        of thirst during concentration.

        I notice in most of my work that unless I breathe
        fully and deeply, there is restriction and sense
        of weariness afterward. A.C. says on the edge
        of breath. Is Spirit breath? My Spirit, no
        doubt, not yet strong enough to work on edge of
        breath; so shall continue my way.

11:07-12   Pranayama. Had to stop, wobbly, yet I feel
        rested and set up.

P.M.
1:15-3:00   Herb Dangerous, Part III.

        30' attempt at visions - nothing.

4:00   Capsule of grass.

        Typed several letters for Lea.

        Dinner at five, grass begins working.

        Hansi says Will with Howard - Peppina comes in
        during this, speaks to Shummie, Hansi stops to
        listen. He finished, I say "Anything going on
        in room certainly distracts Hansi." Lea ans-
        wers: "Yes, Peppina must learn to keep quiet
        when Will is ---- being said, Howie !"
        My downfall due to grass. Lea's ----- ? ?

        Returned to Abbey, lay on couch, essayed "rising
        on planes". Before there was some timidity. Now
        I let myself go, gently and easily. Experienced
        what I assume to be "coolth". Discovered the
        rising was like a breath, expanding naturally so
        far, then returning, again to expand and return.
        Assume advantages to be gained come when one is
        able to remain expanded.
        Noticed, also, the occasional deep breath, this
        breath seeming to permeate me principally along
        front of body, from throat to navel. None along
        back, as I sometimes do in Yoga work.
        Also, seemed to have two minds, the one working
        below - in fact, this mind recited a mantra like
        line, which I knew of course but have forgotten,
        over and over - while the upper went through the

expansion process. When far enough away, I
lost the lower.
Some place in this upper I struck a pitch that
synchronized with physical sex, and I wondered
about striking at will this note, then, after
familiarity, another note an octave higher,
and so on up the scale; this being the "trans-
mutation" advocated by some mystics.

I also seemed to work on lobes, first one then
the other, as though exercising them physically by will.

Feb. 10
A.M.   No work because of grass. Went to Cefalu with
                Lea, had hair cut, ordered sandals.

P.M.
2:00-4:00   Herb Dangerous - conclusion.

4:15-35   Pranayama.
                For first time really good. 10-20

8:50-9:10   I cannot work. Does grass hang on so long?
9:14-29   Pranayama. 10-20

Feb. 11
A.M.
7:30-8:00   French.

10:25-45   Asana.
                Went after leak - negative condition at some
                centre. Got as far as centre of body but
                believe leak is in Mudlahara, or Navel.
10:45-11:05   Dharana.
                Good. Broke at 15'.
11:10-30   Harpocrates.
                Nix.
11:33-48   Pranayama, 10:20
                Think I have the proper muscles in use now.

P.M.
1:20   Think I have definitely located leak - cannot
                properly describe at present, but shall keep a
                weather eye out. Noted it going to Umbilicus
                and since then.

1:35   In order the better to understand the Tarot, I
                work out a problem; and therefore ask "What
                will be the result of my month's retirement?"

                         9 of Pentacles.
                 K'ght of Pen.   2 of Chalices
         6 of Swords   The Lovers
     7 of Wands   _____   King of Pentacles.

                    Complete realization of
                    material gain, good,
                    riches.
                    (Treasuring of Goods)

Knight of Pen.   2 of Chalices - Lord of Love
Unless well dignified   Harmony of masculine and Fem-
(heavy, dull, material.)   inine united. Harmony, pleas-
Laborious, clever in   ure, mirth.
material things.   (Folly, waste, dissipation,
                                   silly actions.)

6 of Swords, Earned Success.   Lovers. Children of the Voice.
Success after anxiety &   Oracles of the Mighty Gods.
trouble; self-esteem, beauty   Inspiration (passive, med-
conceit - sometimes modesty   iumistic); motive power, ac-
therewith; dominance, la-   tion.
bour, etc.

7 of Wands. Valour   King of Pen. Chariot of Earth.
Possible victory, need   Increase of matter - good or
energy & courage. Opposi-   evil; solidifies. Steady, re-
tion, obstacles, difficul-   liable.
ties, yet courage to meet.   (Selfish, animal & material:
(Quarrelling, etc)   stupid.)

(Ill dignified in parentheses. I take it right side well
dignified. Swords inimical to Pentacles, yet Knight must
be more powerful than 6 of Swords? Wands friendly with
Swords and Pentacles. I do not know enough here. But the
left, too, may have a degree of good dignity; at least, I
assume it so. Feb.21)

2:00-3:00   Psychology of Hashish.

3:00-30   Attempt vision. Cannot. Use "Thou who art I"
             and let self go, any place. Travel some dis-
             tance, see golden yellow - wheat straw at child-
             hood home in Pennsylvania. Go through barn,
             visit mulberry tree, etc., wondering why I was
             there. Then get the "likeness" in Lea which
             has cropped up time and again - Laura B. living
             there at present.
                  Silly ass.

7:00-30   "Chicago May" aloud to Lea.

Top of head hurting for hours.

9:00-20	Asana.)
9:20-30	Dharana.)
	Something wrong - think pain causes it.
9:37-10:00	Pranayama, 10-20

Feb.12
A.M.

Peculiar night, waking nearly every hour, but sleeping immediately after.

7:30-8:00 French.

9:10-28   Asana.
Really turned out to be Dharana. I placed myself before an altar candle and became still throughtout being as its unflickering flame;
9:30-45   motionless.
9:30-45   Dharana.
Difficult at first, found door after door closed. Finally stilled myself Buddha-like (visualized) and opened down to sex centre; found some rigidity here, relaxed this; gradually was able to draw in (or so it seemed) new strength, and I seemed on the fringe of something Universal. Too hazy to grasp. Have been after this centre for some days'

15' analyzing and going over interior development, etc.

10:32-42 Pranayama - not steady. But - I am repairing the leak! Praise be for that.

(Ask A.C.:
Was told this symbol means body immortal as well as the soul.)

P.M.
2-4   Psychology of Hashish.

For several days have been concious of forms, interiorly. So far, at least, can eliminate. Is this astral leak?
Also, with resumption of Yoga the top of head is more in evidence. Feel sure I understand this correctly, however.

8:30-50   Asana.
This led up to what at a jump I call "perception."

8:50-9:10   Dharana.
       Still flame of lighted candle steadies and
       quiets me. This has shown me first, that
       there is a kind of buzz going on when I con-
       centrate, as though I were pushing, and, sec-
       ondly, to stop it. May this quality of "per-
       ception" really be focussing for first time?
       In comparison, this is all life, the other
       all dead. For first time candle hopped about,
       but the flame was always steady.

9:20-40   Harpocrates.
       This still baffles me.

9:41-10:03 Pranayama.
       Coughed once, lost 1'.

Feb. 13
A.M.   French. 7:10-8

9:47-10:07 Asana.
       Good.

10:07-28   Harpocrates.
       Put in here to test. Better, as I am fresher?
       Also think I have discovered something else,
       steadying of solar plexus.

10:28-32   Dharana.
       Weaker, because of being third?
       18' Pranayama. A setting up.

P.M.   No work this afternoon, I felt like resting
       mental. Sewed, vigorous and exhilirating Fives
       with Lea.

9:15   Asana. I just pull through.
       Nothing else doing. About an hour ago I took
       a hot lemonade with vodka in it. The same last
       evening and my work seemed improved. This is
       what I get for grabbing a staff on which to
       lean! You walk alone.

9:48-10:08 Pranayama.

Feb.14
A.M.
9:48-10:08 Asana.
       Became still in waiting-without-watching at-
       titude for first time.

10:08-27   Dharana.
       Sometime during first 10' I myself became
       still flame - for what length of time? Delight

```
                      over getting this through me off.  I battled
                      and got still once more toward last few minutes
                      - but only still; no emotion eliminated
10:32-50              Harpocrates.
                      Spotty.
10:54-11:10           Pranayama.
                      Notice present method steadies solar plexus
                      and strengthens.
                      A physical fitness this A.M.


P.M.
12:50                 At Umbilicus, broke silence, when photographs
                      were being taken, with "Well, Shummy"-----

8:40-9:00             Asana.
                      Stupid, a restriction.
9:00-20               Dharana.
                      Ditto.  Finally "look out" with a centre that
                      seems directly upward from soft palate.  Am
                      sometimes conscious of this spot when top of
                      head hurts.  Where is the pineal gland?
9:25-40               Harpocrates.
                      Not satisfactory.
9:45-10:05            Pranayama.

Feb. 15
A.M.                  French, 7:10-50

9:15-33               Asana.
                      Spotty.  Began too soon after Fives?  Shall
                      rest till 9:40
10:00                 Some Dharana.
                      Some discoveries:
                      That this thing in which I do my work
                      is a modification of symbol given me by
                      Fee Wah.  I work from centre of first symbol.
                      2. That what has of late translated itself
                      to me as physical hunger is the solar plexus
                      (?) striving for equilibration; an instrument
                      with all strings tuned (just so some people
                      turn to cigarettes, liquors, etc.; something
                      seeking adjustment is translated into these
                      cravings.)
                        3  That I shall experiment with my break-
                         fast.  The one meal of the day I thoroughly
                         enjoy!

                      For one moment in Dharana I got outer circle
                      stilled, equilibrated; when centre became
```

N.B. Come to think of it, I have never seen that straighter line! There is something there not yet seen by me.

(Feb. 22)

(h, B)

steady flame. This does not describe properly;
I self-controlled, the master, was that circle;
the flame flowing through. Flame passing
through asbestos might describe it.

11:00-20   Pranayama.

P.M.
2:00   Psychology of Hashish.
     (Notice I am at point in Yoga where there is
     tendency to analyze process itself. This
     mentioned in Sanna. Perhaps my "perception"
     of February 12 was after all correct - a
     quality certainly was added never before ex-
     perienced.)

     XVIII Vinnanam. "While there is a particle of
     matter" . . "there is no place for Spirit".
     Shall the world ever have a universal concep-
     tion? I have always said: "Spirit is material
     body of soul".

     "Control of breath and vital nervous currents
     which react in sympathy with it." I now under-
     stand what I am tackling in Pranayama and
     what I mean by "solar plexus".

3:30-50   Attempt vision work. Had just got a gold sun-
     like symbol - on altar? - with 2 tall cylin-
     drical holders either side when a raft of men
     arrived. I hear them moving about - they are
     inspecting all the doors, pictures, etc.,
     making comments.
     The disk is not flat, something is placed on
     the face, or the back is carved away from it.

4:01-21   Pranayama.

7:8   Walk by sea with Lea.

9:30-46   Asana.
     Nothing at all.
9:50-10:10   Harpocrates.
     Nothing. Dry? Heard every little thing - got
     mad at a flea, felt I must get him. Not if
     it kills me! Finally conquered that.

     I cannot work; I blow up like a balloon, all
     wrong. Suspect pork was in Shummie's meat balls
     and pork just will not agree with me.
     (P.S. No pork. She says the soup.).

Feb.10
A.M.
7:10-8:00   French.

9:30-54   Asana)
9:55:10:10 Dharana) Again that quality of "perception".
           Noticed in both these that I left body behind
           and became focussed in more subtle body. Tried
           to see arrangement of gold disk - bars not
           less than six but I think more, may be nine,
           may be still more. In Asana came flat gold
           disk, many pointed, with hieroglyphs; this
           in centre of brilliant white light.
      First gold disk and holders on altar draped in
           white and gold.
    15'   Harpocrates.
           At one time floated in top of egg, but prompt-
           ly put a stop to this.
    10'   Pranayama.

P.M.   A feeling of mental indigestion. So I take a
      walk up the hill, meet the Mississippi Italian,
      drink a bit of his sweet wine, talk a bit, home,
      Fives, supper.

9:15-35   Asana. Good.
           Thoughts: Jefferson, California, Lea's re-
           marks about her recent ordeals. Others, now
           forgotten.
9:35-45   Dharana, spotty.
           Changed position and found I could not work
           so well. I suppose one gets accustomed to
           one particular Asana.
9:50-10:10 Harpocrates. Nothing.
           One long fight to continue.
      Pranayama, 22'

Feb.17
A.M.   Waked up at midnight, horribly cold, feet like
      ice, chills through back. An internal chill, I
      think, as I knew definitely when I would warm
      again.

      A dream, made interesting by the fact that Lea
      saw some time during the night either a black
      bull or black cow, fierce-eyed, long smooth up-
      curved horns. She regarded it only, not ap-
      proaching it.

      First I was on the go, it seemed in trains, but
      I am not sure. Then came to Mary Katherine

washing clothes; a big tub full, she doing this
because woman whose job it was, was elsewhere.
I was on my way to a definite place, at the
place I would find this woman and tell her to go
back to the clothes.

I left M.K. and on my way got a "selfish"
note from myself (?), the sin-complex telling
me I should stay and help sister?. Entered forest and placed myself at foot of an exceedingly
steep ascent, path narrow, tortuous; brambles,
rocks, etc., aplenty. Found myself in small
open space in forest, at great height; here
stood a one-story squat, spreading house. I then
stood on door-step and saw to my right, at corner of house and between it and large tree
(stupidly did not note what kind) a black cow,
Mary Katherine milking it. I approached the
group and was attacked by the cow. First I drew
back toward the house, then went forward - without any fear - and grasped it by both horns,
noting then they were highly polished, thin,
up-curved with sharp points. We struggled, I
telling my sister to go round the house and enter by a rear door (which she did). The cow and
I continued to tussle, I always drawing nearer
the house, she fighting every step. I reached
door-step, worked across threshold and told tall,
thin woman to my left to slide door along. When
I got the horns square across door-way, this
woman slid the door toward me, I let go horns
and pushed door shut completely.

No emotion of any kind.

I convey this to Russell by means of what
French I command (by aid of dictionary) and a
picture. He writes: Isis, 4th puisse de la
Sphinx. And, "A wish phantasy to break the
silence."

10:07-25   Asana.
           Started fair. Two boys rolling iron hoop and
           shouting outside window. At 10:15 I rise &
           close kitchen door. Resume, and during last
           10' for first time get realization of necessi-
           ty for fighting things through. Without this
           training on physical, one could the more easi-
           ly fail elsewhere.
10:30-45   Dharana. Steady flame.
           Worked into what seemed the most tenuous part
           of me yet sensed. First reach by negative
           method. Remain here a bit, negatively, then
           draw back to more familiar territory, rest a
           moment, then slowly work way back, linked up
           with what I have termed "perception".

10:53-11:13 Harpocrates. Nothing.

.11:16-36   Pranayama, 10-20.

P.M.   A feeling of physical fitness - nerve force
            coming into line?

            At table thought of Yi King divination by A.C.
            on his return from Naples. The tiger. Just
            what did that mean? I certainly have clawed,
            bit, scratched and snarled.

2-3   Work on Tarot.

4:10   Shortly after 3 I began Vision work before al-
            tar, Lea in Cefalu. Baron interrupted shortly
            thereafter and insisted on being entertained, I
            with French dictionary in hand. However, I got
            even. Giosue was mentioned and I hauled out
            a gun of A.C.'s to ask about oil, cocked it,
            and he got quite perturbed - in fact, one might
            say he was scairt!

9:06-25   Asana, good.
9:25-45   Dharana
                Asana last 10' painful, but stuck it through.
                Nothing.
9:45-10:05 Harpocrates.
                Nothing.

            5' Pranayama, 10-20
            3'   "   15-30, tickle in throat.

            No stimulant, but feel this evening almost as
            boozy as Lea, who took hashish. Now feel al-
            most light-headed.

Feb. 18
A.M.   Chill started again last night, but I tackled
            and conquered it.

7:30-8:00   French.

9:45-10:05 Asana.
                Force, interest, or whatever it is, continued
                (after getting hold all round) for 15'.
                Thoughts a plenty, of course, but think they
                must be too weak to make sufficient impres-
                sion for me to remember when finished.
10:05-25   Dharana.
                Candle steadily for 10' - lost- battled to

get back, finally did so, when there seemed
more force than during first 10'

10:25-45   Harpocrates.
Lost here after 5', after 10' gone entirely.

18' Pranayama, 10:20
Tried 15-30 but failed.

P.M.
12:50   As to "making" an individual.
It is reasonable to assume that if one can make
one can also break.
The farmer cannot add one jot to his grain of
   wheat. He can provide a suitable sprouting
   place and aid its development, a richer unfoldment.
Again, Burbank has produced new species by
   grafting, and specialization, from two orig-
   inals producing a third. Each original life,
   however, remains the same I assume.
Can one human add one jot to another human?
   Or is it the fuller, richer unfoldment of
   what is already there? And if one can add
   cannot one take from?

These thoughts have come up in connection with
   remarks heard frequently in the artistic
   world - "I made So-and-So", "He made her",
   "She made him what he is". Also the expression "gave her a soul". In the States I always maintained the material was already
   there with which to work. And here, in the
   case of a soul, must not woman herself reach
   out and take what is already hers or may become such? Otherwise, could not a soul be
   engrafted, willy nilly - or, at least, "O,
   all right; if you wish".
Would like this explained in language suitable
   to my mentality.

So would I

2:3:10   Tarot.

3:15-4:00   B U E R - Nix, - unless I once got a huge serpent, writhing, twisting, threatening to
   strike, and again a slender, tall black(?)
   being with an animal head, which head I could
   not distinguish sufficiently to describe.

10' vigorous Pranayama, 10:20
 3'   "   15-30

I feel like smoking opium, so go to it, 8-9.
3 X 58 = 174, *result B opium -*
Somewhere in my being occurs orgasm. Where?
Why? What?

Feb. 19
A.M.

Two other occurrences there were. I did not
write down, wishing to train memory, thinking
them slight. Cannot now remember.

For '30' try work. First think emotional gets
in; then it seems a power I cannot control;
and from this I get into such a state I
lose control.
Opium, no doubt; and I hoped to be the conqueror!

So I lie down and after a time become still.
Then realize a tremendous yearning of body to
unite with mind - a marriage of the two - the
full organ tones of the mind realized by the
forces of the body. Only so shall I be complete. Never before experienced this. Did
I get it last night from opium?

P.M.

Five letters from Paris excite us all. I
write A.C. enclosing letter of introduction
to Dr. DuBouchet.

After Pentagram, read "Flaw in The Defense" &
begin "The E String". Interrupted by Baron.
I study him to-night, and take him to be a
man of some decision and will, behind that
not specially attractive exterior. Speaking
his language fluently one might find something
interesting. Excuse myself at eight and to
my room.

The rock a surprise, if A.C.'a interruption be
correct.
Fee Wah: If you will achieve the "Great Achievement", etc. I assumed this was to take place -
no, that is too definite, I had not thoroughly
analyzed that statement; but I expected something big May, 1920. Nothing happening I
crossed the ocean rather puzzled. Since my
advent in Cefalu, have asked myself if at the
end of the "three years", feeling, however,
this might exclude some things told me.
So, May 1921? After the Achievement; the definite work begins.

Yes:
"nature
vindication -
what I expected.
(Feb. 28)

Or is the "Great Achievement" something else?
And right here, does it mean Good Friday and
Easter Sunday? "Because of your fear we will
spare you this time". I tried then, 1918 but the
agonizing fear!

Feb.20
A.M.

Looking into myself last evening, I decided to
amoke again. This smoking resulted in relaxing all along the line, especially that centre
in the back on a level with the heart - and
then breathing deeply and consciously against
it? through it? with it? - with it, I think,
strengthening and giving it two feet to stand
on.

It does not seem possible that I am ready for
this step - and yet did I expect it to "burst"
upon me a year ago! However, there is 1918
to bolster one. There, after many battles,
did I finally become passionless and say "Into
Thine hands, O God, do I commend my spirit."
So must one enter one's canoe, passionless, empty, and float out over the stream, eyes, ears
and senses alive to what may transpire; so enter the maelstrom, so face the Falls, so drop
with that mighty Niagara, so be churned over
the rocks of the Rapids, finally to enter the
still Lake beyond.
"There must be no turning back; that way lies
destruction."

I now see Lea and I meant the same thing (as
she finally said) in our talk about "letting
go" - my statement that one must consciously
go being, I believe, the stumbling block.
Hello! In this last statement something unearthed of which I thought myself devoid.
VANITY! Bon! So long as you are there, Hail!
Now at last I see your face.

Lea expressed surprised when I said "Failure"
never entered my head. I now realize this
due to fact that "Success" does not enter
either. I simply AM.

E String. Think it splendid; has the picture
quality for which I have been looking - more
than any story yet submitted.

20' Pranayama.

P.M.   No workee - no vision.   Sleep.½ hour.

17' Pranayama.

Hair wash, tub wash, all sorts of washes.

Feb.21
A.M.

Opium. And last night thought after all I made
a mistake in following the impulse. This A.M.
I have an inner happiness, as though the yoke
of the egg were vibrating to some Love theme;
the white, all unconscious of what has taken
place, nevertheless being permeated by it; the
mind steadied and given a sense of calm no-
bility.

For future reference I would like here to put
down my interpretation of "I will breed from
her a child more powerful than all the Kings
of the earth." This should have been entered
in my record when Comment was being prepared,
because then it was this thought came to me.
From rounding out of Scarlet Woman, through
Beast and otherwise, through Strength and Love
developed in her, shall she reach the Marriage
Bed of Aiwass. From that Bed shall be born
the child of R.H.K.
The Law is for all, yet it seems "classes" at
the present are for Book of Law, the proud
and mighty, the fierce and strong, etc., etc.
Kings rule the masses. The child of R.H.K and
S.W. shall reach the masses.
Thus bringing both poles, classes and masses,
into contact, making a complete whole.

"Clothed with the Sun". The Christ of the new
dispensation shall be a woman." Is there any
connection here (assuming Kingsford's vision
to be correct) - except, that she was in line
with the masses - or, that she could grasp only
the Feminine and not the Masculine; that she
got the half and not the whole.

I think I have the lesson of the opium. Again
was I concentrating exclusively on the mental,
forgetting the other so necessary angles of
my being; again ill-balancing myself.

P.M.
1:30-3:05   E String.

3:10-3:05	Vision - nothing.
3:30-4:00	Sleepless last night, a nap.

Time and time again going through exercise
of strengthening a subtle body to withstand
shock and attack, it seems to me. Definitely
stopped at 4, so rise for Pranayama.

4:06-26	Pranayama, 10-20
	3' Pranayama, 15-30, less 5"

9:35-55	Asana.
9:55-10:10	Dharana.

Both passionless, colourless, it seemed with
body only - no mind.

10:17-37	Prsnayama, 10-20

Feb.22
A.M.

Smoked half an hour last night. Afterwards a
partial consciousness of the fear which all
good Egos experience at thought of being
smashed to smithereens. To my mind this
links up with work of this afternoon.

9:35-53	Asana.

A holding still, controlling of nervous organism?

9:54-10:13	Dharana.

A hanging on to lighted candle by this same
organism. (I suppose these entries sound in-
sane, but down they must go as I analyze them.
Some day I shall understand.)

I lose sense of physical being entirely at
times, but thoughts dim and hazy float by at
intervals.

Outward disturbed by water boiling over, but
found I did not lose inner sight, though much
weakened.

Pranayama, 5'.

P.M.
1:30

Typed on own record 11-12, 1-1:30. Resting.

1:30-3:15	E String.

3:30-4:00	Nature is certainly smoothing me out - must

have snarled myself up somewhere. This nap
leaves me ironed out.

4:08-25	Pranayama. 10-20

8:00-18   Asana.
           Good. Broke once, so turned light of lamp
           so I could see watch.

8:20-35   Dharana.
           Bad. Could not get hold. Finally got despe-
           rate, grabbed and held whatever I could.

8:40-59   Harpocrates.
           A sitting still, mind in chaos at first (due
           to above grabbing?), then settled into a
           heavy, slow rhythm, which I could eliminate
           only at intervals.

9:05-20   Pranayama.
           Throat began to trouble, tickle. Surprised
           I got this far - everything rebelled. Freudian
           throat? Wish phantasy?

10-11   Opium, smoking slowly, few pipes.

11:40   Went "out" for a moment.
           Was standing in Temple room, against wall between
             kitchen and wine room, near Circle, saying a
             ritual. I got to "Holy Guardian Angel, whose
             child I am", when I went out on a flash of
             fire that was not fire, though there seemed a
             moment's warmth. Instant thought: "I wonder
             if A.C. would approve?" Then let myself go.
             Went upward with a great rushing of wind, rose
             higher and higher, then returned, easily.
             After first speed, noted things in space, but
             my vision weak.

12:50   Why the hurling of self against something, I
             know not what. With self there was conscious-
             ness of water.

1:00   A face - cannot tell whether animal or man, or
             combination of both; intent eyes regarding me
             fixedly, questioningly - a look of "Will you
             or will you not?" I look steadily, imperson-
             ally. It disappears. An out-post, stationed
             there to watch and report to an hierarchy, it
             seemed to me.

9:45-10:05 Asana.
           Took hold again with "nervous organism".
           Nerves in legs jumping. Steadied them, and
           controlled nerves throughout.

10:07-26   Dharana.
           Same nervous organism, plus plane of vibration
           of last evening. Where is this? What is it?
           Stopped this intermittently, to have it jump
           back again.

Pain in legs frightful last 5' - left leg numb to hip.

10:33-50   Pranayama, 10:20

The immediately present work seems confined to establishing equilibration of nervous organization, magnetic centres, etc.

One gun cleaned!

P.M.
1-2   Type on record.

2-3   E String. Nothing accomplished; feel dull.

3:00-3:40   Nap.

3:40-4:10   B U E R. Silly ass to continue on this when I am and have been convinced for some time that it is not my will at present. That force needed elsewhere? In all Yoga work am hammering away on magnetic centres, nervous control, etc.- now that I know what I am after. Of course, this will not continue forever - indeed, may change to-morrow!

10' Pranayama.

Feb.24
A.M.   At Fives last evening noted weariness of body. At dinner decided to quit opium, 5 nights of it. At 6:30 decided to go to bed, did so, Tarot a bit. At eight turned out light. At 6:10 this A.M. waked. Some sleep!

9:35-51   Asana.
        Conscious of ear-drums, physical shakiness. Finished vigorous game with Russell at 9:15. Work attempted too soon?
9:55-10:10   Dharana.
        Difficult - finally landed. Interrupted by Giovanni's brother at the door, thumping and I, not knowing who it might be, went to door!

Notice thoughts increasingly difficult to banish, i e, they seem more strenuous. Noticed lack of inclination to work. Ear-drums also.

10:15-35   Harpocrates.
        First 10' nothing - second 10 a "breathing" along entire spine; centre between shoulders, solar plexus, throat, then full body. Would I

Could so breathe against my brains!

10:40-48   Pranayama.
            Body wobbly, shake somewhat; but feel splendid.

I am beginning to sense emotions, thoughts of
  a character humiliating to myself, thoughts
  and emotions never before touched. And yet
  am I also conscious of habitation where all
  is peace, serenity; as of the serene expanse
  of sky, luminous, impersonal, above clouds of
  more or less density or murkiness.
And right here I am taking satisfaction in
  that fact --- Bang! Off goes his head!
  Caught you that time, Mr. Sin Complex. Why
  should I not take satisfaction in knowing that
  "somewhere the sun is shining", and be able
  to repose in that upper mind experienced in
  hashish? Albeit, I can understand, of course,
  that for special development this might or
  could be cut off from one's consciousness,
  and one be left "without a leg to stand on".

P.M.
3:30   Left Abbey at 1 for a climb up the hill - a
            new walk and one very beautiful. Return at
            three. Turkish coffee, and now work of some
            kind.

            Mess around, and finally type on record till
              4:50

6:00   Am wondering if I will be rid of my Old Man of
            the Sea after May. Or, shall he ride me for
(No, believe   three years lest I depart the Path, as I did
he will move to once in California: wiped the slate clean.
left entirely to Had I not staggered back when I could get back,
me Feb. 8)   verily would there have been "destruction" in-
            deed.

10:30   Again "spilled the beans", grabbing Shummy and
            dancing with her after Pentagram; and then
            starting with Genesthai to hear Lea in a loud
            voice reading the Abbey record.
            (But I know which is the better dancer, I do!)

            Later I read aloud Revelations, the two of us
            cudgelling our brains. Amen.

Feb.25
A.M.
1:20   Chill - which I have struggled against at fre-
quent intervals since retiring - so long as
I lie on my back, which I will do. What was
it I worked out by reason of this? Something
to do with Abbey, Lea and myself. A flea
walking on my back brought me to and I did
not at first know whether it was my back or
Lea's on which the flea walked.

Very good
=

Heard distinctly "Eric, Eric" outside window,
thinking some-one at peasant's door. It developed into the dog coughing.

3:40   Still awake.
And remember that I should have entered heretofore fact that I have not been conscious of
beings interiorly for many days.

Sleep at four, peasants wake me 6:30

9:00   Spoke one sentence in English to Shummy at Fives.
And did not even notice that I did so, so
weary am I in mind and body.
But, were my subconscious thoroughly charged
with the necessity for silence, would this
happen?

The wakefulness served its purpose. All night
I lay, muscles rigid and in pain from uric
acid. This thing must go else must my work
go.

10:20   Note to English Pharmacy.
I try work and cannot - lifeless, body stiff and
numb.

P.M.
4:10   All guns finished - one hour on each! Which is
all right provided they be done properly.

Went after opium pipes this morning, to cement,
clean, etc. Red one full of long mould. No
wonder it stank.

8:35-8:55   Asana.
Under all circumstances, fair I suppose.
Try Dharana - nothing doing.

Feb.26
A.M.
7-7:40   French.

```
10:00-20    Asana
10:20-37    Dharana
10:39-59    Harpocrates.
            In all three quality to stay put; i e,ability
            to remain intact although swept away by a
            whirlwind.  This has led up from control of
            "nervous organism .
11:01-21    Pranayama, 10-20  Almost quit after 10'

P.M.        Never in my life have I been so continuously
            cold, day after day, week in and week out.
            Must have eaten up a lot of force resisting it.

            2 hours E String - think I have this now.

            40' concentration - messed up.

            I certainly am in a mood.  I scorn A.C.'s "so-
            cial freedom" of Cefalu.  The freedom of the
            prison yard!  And all the time I know that one
            can be free in a narrow cell.

9:07-25     Asana.
9:25-35     Dharana
9:35-53     Harpocrates.
            The proverbial pulling of teeth.  Haven't any
            idea whether anything accomplished.

Feb.27
A.M.        Wakeful night.

9:52-10:12  Asana.
10:12-23    Dharana
            In Asana taking full breath occasionally.
            A taking hold by an exceedingly thin thread,
            hard to hold.  I am wondering if this might
            be the exercise of weak spots to bring up to
            normal of others.
10:28-50    Harpocrates.
            Nothing.
            10' Pranayama, rather shaky.

P.M.        Letter to A.C.

            Fussing about - resting the Seventh Day, I
            reckon.

8:58-9:18   Asana.
            Went to this with renewed energy.
9:18-38     Dharana.
            Hard to hang on last 5' - legs aching, flea
            walking.
```

9:20-10:00 Harpocrates.
        Improvement here. Instead of being one with
        Silence I was trying to pierce that Silence.
        6' Pranayama, 10-20
        Do not know why I should be wobbly to-day.

Feb.28
A.M.   Another sleepless night - though no strain.

        Night before last I saw large open square,
        formed by intersection of four streets. Three
        men dashed, in autos, into this square from
        one street, attempting to pass down street
        at right angles. All three, in turn, crash-
        ed on turn, mangled, bleeding, unconscious.
        At third mishap I ran for doctor, found nurse
        who said doctor was already there and that
        first man attempted suicide. No one killed.
        In this emotion of shock.

        Last night, walking down west side of Broad-
        way, Camille A of Los Angeles on my left,
        back of us balance of party (three, I think)
        and of the Brotherhood. She suddenly darted
        ahead of me and threw herself in front of a
        horse-driven vehicle, attempting suicide.
        She wore a one-piece robe, colourless though
        not white, deep cream. I reached her after
        she had been picked up, not dead. She came
        to and stood, arrested. There welled through
        my being a profound sympathy and deep love,
        and I stooped and kissed her hands reverently.
        Should say I expected the "members" to follow
        up, but they passed out of sight, taking no
        note of the occurrence.

        Controlled "dream". Afterwards took hold
        again and again with centre used for this
        control - to strengthen?

9:55-10:15 Asana.
        Good.
10:15-33   Dharana. Gold disk.
        Good when obtained - lost frequently. Struck
        the shorter breath. Must note this.
        Wondered if white & gold altar, gold disk,
        &c., connected with white & gold door named
        by me Melchisedeck.
        Try Harpocrates.

Yesterday wondered about shakiness. Chump!
My diet of bread & milk for past two days,
with a bit of cheese, a cup of wine last night.
Notice a change in uric acid. Will go after
this for a few days and then, plus salol, may
eliminate much and go onto the Rock with a
sounder & stronger physical.

10' Pranayama.

P.M.   "Sooner or Later" scenario - this does not im-
          press me as favorably as heretofore.

3:15-45   Concentration.

3:45-4:15 Nap - mind feels like a yawn.

          7' Pranayama. Bread & milk.

7:30   Mind condition result of diet, I think. Shall
          eat to-morrow.

8:05-25   Asana.
            Good.
8:25-45   Dharana.
            My first victory over physical. At 9:35
            thought I could not pull through another 5',
            every pulse thumping, all nerves. At 9:40
            edge dulled into a muffled ache & I was able
            to concentrate mental. New spasms lurking
            elsewhere, I suppose.
8:47-9:05 Harpocrates.
            Gone entirely after 8' & could not recover.

Mar. 1
A.M.
9:50-10:10 Asana
            Continuous battle with emotional & at the
            end lost out.
10:10-28 Dharana
            Difficult, but finally got rid of emotional.
10:30-50 Harpocrates
            Did not get into this till 10:40, then
            fringe only, losing frequently.
          5' Pranayama.

I resume ordinary fare again. My body feels
as though tired by violent exercise. This diet

proposition I cannot think good for me. Tried
it before, and it failed - but then it was of
a more violent nature.

P.M. Walk after tiffen - return at 2:10

E String one hour.

Vision attempted - nothing. Then lay down &
smoothed out what seemed mental snarls.

20' Prayanama, 10-20

8:28-47 Asana.
  Good beginning, weakened toward end.
8:47-9:05 Dharana.
  Spotty.
9:08-27 Harpocrates.
  Think I am getting into the "waiting" attitude.
8' Pranayama.

Mar.2
A.M.
7:45 Past four nights waked at 2, lying awake till
after 4; last night dozing between 2 & 3,
peasants keeping me from sleep 6-7, sleep then
somewhat.
 Last night I was "cast down" - a dream, and
I attempted no control! After two years without a slip. This waked me at 2
 In various naps after 4 I witnessed crowds
love-making (my second night like this), myself coming in for a prolonged kiss in front
of folks, which embarrassed me hugely.
 At another time it fell to me, for some reason
to speak to a blond of about 16, who was making love to a dark man - to call her attention
to two side of love, one benefitting, the other
wasting. She promptly began making love to me.
I put her aside, when she fell upon a dark-
haired girl to my right.
 Some place in here A.C.'s paint brushes, all
white, and a practical joke on a fat man, who
thereby paid a large bill not his to pay.

10:00-20 Asana.
  Good. Stood on circle of Temple with nervous organism only, I should say. These

MSS

practises are steadying me.

10:20-38   Dharana.
    Down to brass tacks. Finally landed on spot
    always indulging in exhaustive rhythm.

10:40-11   Harpocrates.
    Like acting: more art required to do nothing
    than something.
    13' Pranayama.

P.M.
1:45   Heavens! A degree of fitness in my head -
    better than at any time since May, 1918.

2:00-3:30 E. String.

3:40-4:10 Vision.
    Too indistinct to decipher. Some confusion
    about a black snake. Also conscious of
    brilliant green of or on a being passing me.
    Finally got golden-yellow serpent, with rich
    seal-brown circles on back, standing on its
    tail. Think head puff adder type.

4:15-30   Pranayama.

6:30   Shummie & I both come to grief over Bysshe
    & milk!

9:05-25   Asana
9:25-44   Dharana.
    Hammering away.
9:45-10:05 Harpocrates.
    Tired but stuck it through, getting & losing
    constantly.
    Body will not Pranayam.

Mar 3
A.M.   French ½ hr.

10:00-19   Asana
10:20-40   Dharana.
    Get into these well at times- fluctuating,
    of course. No mental last 5' Dharana.
10:41-11: Harpocrates
    Never get as deeply into this as A G D. All
    gone last 5'.
    8' Pranayama.
    My body acts as though stimulated. I lose
    muscular control & get shaky.

P.M.   I committed an error this noon in saying Adoration. Lea prepared for Palermo, remaining at Abbey for tiffen. I assumed the same regime would hold as held when she was in Palermo with A.C. - that the Adorations & Pentagram by Alostrael meant while she was present in Abbey and that in her absence in Palermo, or elsewhere, the Abbey was not to go without Pentagram & Adoration. A good thing this came up, otherwise I would have held Pentagram this evening.

Read "Shadow Line".

Think I am touching the surface at intervals - emerging from the depths of negativity.

9:00   I am nerve weary to-night. Shall not do Yoga but will take Liber Aleph.

Mar.4
A.M.   Waked at 2:45 - could not sleep, read Liber Aleph. Slept toward 6, to be waked intermittently by peasants.

9:30-50   Asana.
    Dispersion all right!
9:50-10:07 Dharana
    Got back in some degree & for first time fought way back to focussing point without a moment's relaxing after losing; i e, the mind winking an eye to relieve strain.
10:10-30 Harpocrates
    Got this but slightly 2 or 3 times. After 15' thought I could not go on, stopped, then resumed, but really was a sitting still.

P.M.   Letter to M K W

Genesthai disappoints me at last. When A.C. & Lea were in Palermo he read Magick, did an Invocation to Mercury alone in Temple. I dismissed this, however, with Do as thou wilt and understanding a hungry man filching food. To-day (Lea left this A.M. for Palermo) neither he nor Shummy come for Fives. At lunch I had to write for water. He came, filled bucket, then wrote "When buckets are empty get Peppina to fill." Does he lack a sense of honour or self-respect?

1921

I discovered a dull edge on his sense of responsibility when he rattled off "Sure, I'll
be godfather to them (Hansi & Howard) or any
other."

2:50   For 50' seeking for   in Sepher Sephi-
roth. Vision & Voice, "..and the name
is broken", etc. Cannot locate, nor does my
sum of these letters help me.

3:10-40   Vision. Fumbled around for some time, then
settled into a definite "waiting" - holding
the harp of mind still, receptive for slightest
whisper. Believe this should be my present
work.

3:45-4:00   Pranayama, 10:20
    Cannot understand why this has become more
    difficult than heretofore.

The Baron came to the Abbey. I despise these
surreptitious rappings, these sneak-thief
methods. I remained in the kitchen, silent
(ha! ha!), and he went away. Now, what? Do
him good anyway, for he heard me before I heard
him.

Glanced at Profits of Religion.

8:40-9:00   Asana
9:99-17   Dharana.
    A horrid, clamped-down feeling I could not
    overcome.
9:20-40   Harpocrates.
    Nothing, head bad.

    4' Pranayama. Dry spot in my throat, I am
    coughing.

Mar.5
A.M.   8 nights of wakefulness from 2 on, sleeping
    intermittently in late morning. What is the
    cause?

9:35-55   Asana
    Discovered reason for "clamped down" feeling
        - wrong focussing apparatus.
9:55-10:13 Dharana
    Followed up preceding & got something. Think
    I sense another phase of disk beyond symbol

	of Yoni, but incompletely else could I de- scribe.
10:17-36	Harpocrates. Preceding helped this. Hanging on to vis- ualization my mistake here? Put one'self into egg, complete picture, then let go & WAIT. 8' Pranayama. Have this, too; heretofore muscles of nos- trils helping to control expulsion of breath. Diaphragm, go it alone!
P.M.	No; it is not the "Great Attainment". I see the whole thing at last - the building; the details of the furnishings will come later.
	30' of stupidity with the Baron! I can't talk, therefore he can't talk: why sit and stare?
	A "Note on Genesis" in connection with 2911. Yassir, I now know all about it!
	Begin Salol for acid. Lea back, we "chatter".
8:00-20	Asana. Do not know.
8:20-32	Dharana. Hit once.
8:35-48	Harpocrates. Bum.

Mar 6
P.M.

3:55	Took a walk up over the hills this morning, peevish, I reckon, hoping to straighten out self. Bowden arrives & we entertain him af- ter tiffen, Fives & a walk. Hope it proves a profitable change. This sleeplessness has to be corrected.
10:30	Bowden leaves at 6:30 Lea & I finish evening together trying Geomantic Figures & Tarot. Will have to do better than this or I will never earn a nickel! Gave her the devil all round.
	A complete day of change; therefore rest?

Mar 7
A.M.   Same kind of night.

10:07-25   Asana
                 Quieted down somewhat in this - got one
                 glimpse of Impersonal Mind, and realized
                 these past 8 or 9 nights' lack of sleep re-
                 sult of personal mind, which then seemed so
                 petty.
10:25-44   Dharana
                 Stuck to the guns, O yes - working in my
                 room. Peasants jabbering, etc., could hold
                 gold disk but it was like looking at a page
                 without reading a word.
10:45-11:03 Harpocrates
                 Principally a getting into larger fields.
                 At one time became egg, water & everything
                 in picture.

            Realized I have admitted a detrimental current,
            but do not know how or where. Have been try-
            ing Simon Iff. Cannot do this, improper un-
            derstanding, no doubt. Work this A.M. has
            helped, I hope.

            20' Pranayama.
            Greater freedom of physical channels.

            I wonder if it is possible for one to tighten
            the blood vessels. For several years I was
            constipated. Then one night in California,
            waking, somehow I discovered that I was hold-
            ing my bowels rigid. Discovered quite some
            time before that, that I held my stomach so.

P.M.   Some time back Lea mentioned sexual "restric-
            tions" by the Beast. The matter revolved
            itself in my mind, because of the Oath, for,
            to an outsider, it suggests attachment. Can
            the Beast limit the Scarlet Woman sexually,
            no matter what the pretext or reason? May
            the Scarlet Woman limit herself?
            If so, it might be the loop-hole: otherwise
            wretched Scarlet Woman if -------

            Draft an essay on Abbey.

            20' bum concentration.

            23' Pranayama, 10-20

9:50-10:10 Asana
Got at first, afterwards lost entirely.
Broke posture once.

10:10-20 Dharana
Poor. Head aching, ears buzzing. (From capsule of salol taken ½ hr before beginning work?)

10:30-45 Harpocrates.
Hurrah! Worked entirely outside physical, for I got away from head-ache, buzzing, etc. It can be done. (Horrible discovery!)

I have been going over Genesthai's stupor from a wine indulgence - "drunk" Shummy calls it. Considering the regime under which he works, this is small enough. I have gone over Lea's battles (as told me & what I witnessed), Shummy's, and my own. Each several months reaching the crest, after which, though one did fall back, it was but momentary, so to speak. Genesthai's appetites his fight at present? And why shorten the time for him?

1921

Mar 8
A.M.

Retired at 11, waked 2:10. Lay awake till 5, head aching, from salol? Then wept a bit in weariness. Disturbed sleep balance of A M.

Have worked out in Yoga something I do not yet understand. In December said I was working on astral. Recently have written "nervous organism". With this in mind have worked from throat downward, spot between shoulders, solar plexus, hip section and, just recently, down legs and into feet. Since steadying nerves in legs & feet? - since working on astral of legs & feet? - since appealing to intelligence in cells of legs & feet? - or whatever it may be, I seem to have come to a clearing in the forest, for from this section of body do I look out over space - it takes me from the personal to the Impersonal, first sensed in this way yesterday A.M. in Asana.

No salol to-day. Shall discontinue 2 days, then continue with 2 capsules a day.

15' Asana (attempt)
10' Dharana - nothing.

1921

P.M.
4:00

Have the gods come to the rescue?
After tiffen I type on E String till 2:30, then
decide to woo sleep. I lie in mental turmoil till 3:40. I assume body fell asleep
at 3.45. I was busy, in a way I cannot recall, then occurred the following:
A man seated in north of Circle, a man with
whom I am in some way acquainted, he hailing
from Australia. I near box in West and between West & North. Some one seated in West.
My feet on white circle. Something, Invocation I think going on. Man then started
formula alone, words I do not recall if, indeed, I understood them at the time. I then
observed he changed from apparently simply
saying the words to a very definite method,
which required conscious use of soft palate,
I believe - this way bringing much magic to
his aid. I then noticed a most intense atmosphere, more & more charged, till I said
to myself I cannot continue in this current-
I must leave Circle. All pressure was through
or against what I believe similar to "nervous
organism" on interior plane - or was it the
same?

New current started February 25? Since then I
have been sleepless & the last few days there
has been most distinct pressure and anything
arising in me, involuntarily, has been antag-
onistic to A.C. Lea suggested subconscious
fear of Rock. But after diligent inquiry
during these last days I do not think so. It
simply means an opening has been afforded &
I have been attacked.

Later: A connection here with opium occurrence
of February 22?

(P.S. Mar 15. Understand reason for this attack. I was "leaning", waiting to be led:
I had to be left "on the rocks" and attacked
that I might realize this.)

Mar 9
A.M.

16' Asana.
A wading around, it seemed, trying to under-
stand.
Try Dharana - all messed up.
Shall try to locate difficulties during day.

Should say that I retired at 9 and slept well
    although waking frequently, sleeping soon
    after and no exhaustive wakefulness. Tried
    Pranayama, but failed on that. Something
    about me is very tired.

P.M.
8:30   Start opium: I wish to know about the diffi-
                culty, although I shall not make a practise
                of drugs during this training period.

Mar 10
A.M.   Whether or no difficulty solved, I feel better.
                Smoked till 9:30. We wondered if a drop of
                heroin might help - took it - no, mind ex-
                tremely alert, and what came into it of val-
                ue, if so, passed at moment of birth. It
                kept me awake till mid-night and I dreamed &
                dreamed of being chased by some one. I ran
                down many flights of stairs, finally leaped
                from floor to floor, into taxis & out again.
                At last, said to myself: this is tiring, it
                must stop. It stopped.
                Yesterday I began wondering if I were impatient
                for the Retirement - if there was that in me
                that wished to jump in & experience something
                similar to May, 1918 - the torture chamber.
                Lea says pleasure & pain the same. Is this
                in me also?

9:40-58   Asana.
10:00-20   Dharana
                Do not know whether anything accomplished.
10:20-40   Harpocrates
                Ditto. Here toward end had to fight peev-
                ishness.
                20' Pranayama, 10-20

P.M.   Finished typing E String.

3:15-35   BUER. Cannot even visualize Talisman.
                10' concentration.
                20' Pranayama. 10-20

8:10-30   Asana
8:30-50   Dharana
                Did I accomplish aught? No visualization,
                just a hanging on to nothing - or did I hang
                on?
8:51-9:10   Harpocrates
                Rigid body, which may be right. Rigid mind.

1921

Did not go as deep within as heretofore. This
thing of not knowing whether one is all right
or all wrong! I feel like smashing the china.

15' Pranayama, 10-20

2 capsules salol to-day & shall continue.
Improvement.

Mar 11
A.M.

Pentagram.
Another fight is on? Back of my eye-lids,
it seems, a gold cross with the rose, perfectly formed, on a blue field or nimbus.
Afterwards blue outlined in gold - not so
sure of this as I tried to concentrate elsewhere & rid myself of it.
This the sort of vision I was specially warned
about May, 1918. Not the inner vision.
Because of this, I have been trying to locate
Lea's visions, though it may be her way to
get them any place, anyhow.
BUT - come to think of it - I was told "not
to watch"!! Chump.
In this way three heads appeared before me
at that time, "Fee Wah, Alester, and that
one that called himself Christ".

9:30-46   Asana.
Suppose I accomplished something as I did
not hear Seth bawling.
9:49-10:10 Dharana
One continuous fight between "Tipperary" & Seth.
10:10-27   Harpocrates
Ditto. So tired I could bawl. Think self-
pity here; otherwise no emotional re-action.
20' Pranayama, 10-20

A dream last night, which seems to smack of
Good Friday and Easter Sunday. I start on
the back of some animal on a trip into China,
either on a Wednesday or a Friday. I ask of
a man (in front of me on this animal?) "We
return to-morrow evening?" "No; we go on to
Mexacali and get back here the third day."
(Out west Mexacali is known as a hell-hole)

P.M.   25' Vision - nothing.
20' Pranayama, 10-20

1921

7:52-8:12 Asana.
8:12-32   Dharana
           February I seemed to do this work with more
           freedom. Now there seems no will working
           to hold on by.
8:32-51   Harpocrates.
           I don't know.
           20' Pranayama.

Mar 12
A.M.   30' Vision. Nothing.

           Pentagram.
           A symbol shaped like Saturn, same colours
           as yesterday A.M. Symbol here outlined in
           ox-blood red, blending into central colour,
           which I call gold. Symbol in nimbus or halo
           of Uranus blue. After a time dot appeared
           in centre. Colour of symbol changed, to
           blue, I think outlined in same red, and gold
           bar came into ends of ring. But I was strug-
           gling not to look and attention was much di-
           vided. The outline of red blends into yel-
           low - line not sharply defined.

           Physically weary in Fives, I held out for oc-
           cult reasons, and finished well. Genesthai
           and I well matched at times.

9:47-10:07 Asana
           When starting red-yellow fire, deep within
           me. Stopped this at once.
10:07-27   Dharana
           Must be accomplishing something, as at times
           I can eliminate all sound & pain of ankle
           bone & legs - this A.M. latter so bad I
           could unfold but very gradually.
10:30-50   Harpocrates
           Do not seem to get into this at all.
           20' Pranayama, 10-20

P.M.   Letter to A.C.

           Walk with Lea

           Going over Goetia sigils.

8:05-24   Asana
8:25-44   Dharana
8:45-10:04 Harpocrates.
           Body aching frightfully, but stuck it out.
           20' Pranayama.

192'

Mar 13
A.M.
6:30-55   BUER - Nix.

                 Pentagram.
                   Messed up - lost something through determin-
                   ation to focus elsewhere.
                 First a top, then head to top, then addition
                   to right of top. Here confusion began.
                   Same colours as heretofore.
                 And am not sure whether terminations of stems
                   triangles or oblongs, but think triangles.

Think this
arrangement.

9:58-10:18 Asana
                   Hung on here.
10:18-28   Dharana
   --   One continuous fight. Seth bawling as when
                   worried by peasant's dog, I wanting to take
                   a stick and beat dog. Then arguing, "This
                   is good training, one must learn to walk,
                   silent, among the shrieks of struggling
                   humanity". Did not lose picture & finally
                   got into it, more or less - principally less.
10:40-59   Harpocrates
                   Don't know if anything accomplished.
                 20' Pranayama, 10-20. Broke once.

P.M.   Walk along hillside overlooking sea.

3:45   Baron & painter just left. Went over house
                   with them & Lea.

                 I search everywhere for Marbas sigil I made
                   last evening - not to be found.

                 25' with white triangle in blue field. Cannot
                   visualize it, but in beginning apple tree in
                   full bloom.

                 17' Pranayama.

8:02-20   Asana
8:20-40   Dharana
                   Torture of body & mind. Everything internal
                   rigid till half-way through, then got better
                   hold. Use "God moves along line of least
                   resistance" to get into shape.
8:45-9:05 Harpocrates
                   "The minutes drag like prisoners' weeks".
                   After 8' thought I just could not continue.
                   Then whipped mind into holding picture -
                   nothing more.
                 20' Pranayama, 10-20

1921

Mar 14
A.M.
5:15-40   Vision - nothing. Again sense of apple tree
          in blossom.

          Pentagram.
            Last evening decided to regard impersonally
            any symbol & see what happened. This A.M.
            did so, indistinct, looked like small dumb-
            bell, long bar. Same colours - red outline
            blending into gold centre. Not nearly as
            distinct as heretofore.

9:26-43   Asana
            Seemed to use head region for first time -
            nothing last 3'
9:45-10:07 Dharana
            Had to break this for laundry woman - knew
            this when starting. Again head; this time,
            I think, all faculties under will, positive,
            with central part receptive.
10:10-30 Harpocrates
            Nothing at all last 3' - with lapses before,
            of course.
          Find myself using affirmations to compel
          obedience - "I am", "I will stand here", "I
          will regard", etc.

          20' Pranayama.

P.M.   1 hr 15' walk.

          Make another Marbas Talisman. Also Halohel.

          23' Marbas.
            On first closing eyes after studying Talis-
            man would see before me broad low-lying
            light bldg., Egyptian door-way, steps lead-
            ing up - these length of bldg. So I walked
            up & put Talisman on that door. Inside dark-
            ness.
          Then did I stand on edge of an abyss, dark?
            Tried to bring someone out of this but failed.
            Then found myself in full sunlight on edge,
            air fresh. I passed through air & sunlight
            of a wonderful freshness & clarity
          Was this occasioned by "cause and cure of
          disease"?

          Halohel.
            Same bldg appeared. Got rid of it. Went
            straight up and up, but seemed to pass earth
            and things of earth. Finally came to stone
            flagging, at which I stopped. After a time

1921

a tall man of great dignity appeared. (Did
I first see an old woman, bent?) A man of
45 or 50, a head piece with 2 horns, and ap-
parel falling from the shoulder.

These things not nearly so distinct as Shaddai.

Shall use Halohel A.M., Marbas P.M.

26' Pranayama, 10:20

8:00-20   Asana
Went into this easily, but after 8' battled
ticking of watch continuously.

8:20-40   Dharana
No mental concentration last 3'. Body after
8' began howling, in rising crescendo till
getting to a point where muscles became sort
of gassy, bones hurting, & I expecting
spasmodic jerking any moment - in legs only.

8:45-9:05 Harpocrates
This worse than cross-legged, for the pain
of torso makes breathing jerky at times.
Got control last 5' of body, but no silence.
20' Pranayama, 10-20
Although I swore I would do but 15 - Amen!

Mar 15
A.M.
6:00-24   HALOHEL
Nothing.

Pentagram
Think I now have way to these particular
visions. All outer sheaths, "planes of consciousness"?, held still & these things float
before me. This A.M. a combination of Rose
Cross and Saturn. Same colours, blue nimbus
square this time.

Mental control my biggest battle ground, at
present.

9:40-10:00 Asana
Nothing mental last 3'. Body easy, possibly
because at no time intense stillness. I in
my room, peasants outside, Lea preparing for
painters.

10:00-20 Dharana
Considerable battle with physical vision.
Also at 10:30 I suddenly stopped & removed
my sandal, rather automatically. Herein
lies value of "Silence"

Mar. 1921

10:20-40   Harpocrates
        Got this intermittently; I think the correct
        way.

        When starting, the emotional, the whimpering,
          coiled in the subterranean passages, ready
          to spring at the slightest opportunity - all
          through Asana & Dharana, in fact.

        22' Pranayama, 10-20

P.M.   Letter to M.K.W. enclosing E String.

        Typed rough draft of article in re Abbey.

        MARBAS
          The Egyptian bldg again. I put it aside as
          I willed to do Marbas.
        On edge of a vast crater: I stood far above the
          sea. I seemed to slid down this, deliberate-
          ly, while standing on the brink.
        Started over again.
          A low gate in a wall. Put sign on it and
          entered. Before me, up a pathway, a small
          bldg., white-washed it seemed but not fresh.
          Open doorway, darkness inside. I called.
          Many things I could not see rushed out past
          my feet, small things I could not see flew
          past my head. I entered & through blackness
          what seemed a wretched man creature, whisk-
          ers, fangs, matted hair, was stowed away in
          a crevice. Could do nothing else, so left.
        Made another attack, going through large door.
         A giant joined me, I came about to his knee.
        We walked. I saw foot and leg as of a croc-
        odile. Nothing more.

        Am I fooling myself?

        20' Pranayama.

8:05-25   Asana
          Start out well enough, but to hang on!
8:25-45   Dharana
          Hard, hard work; right thigh feeling as if
          it would break.
8:47-9:07 Harpocrates.
          I don't know - nothing, I guess.
          20' Pranayama, 10-20

1921

Mar 16
A.M.
4:00-20   HALAHEL

I travel, yes; seem to rise at times - always a sense of earth; ground, I mean, as distinguished from rocks.

9:30   For first time, am beginning to feel a physical reaction, as of strain.

9:40-10:00 Asana
10:00-20 Dharana

Am wondering about this "automatic rigidity", "corpse rigid". People of perfect concentration work with relaxed bodies. God moves along line of least resistance.

It is only a stage
half-way

10:20-40 Harpocrates.
I don't know.

I'm tired.

20' Pranayama.

P.M.   Lay 2 hours in hot sun on court.

15' Egyptian house. Door massive, of polished mahogony colour, house cement, thick walls. Could get nothing, then whole house, terrace & I rose, and kept on going. Found myself becoming, as I thought dizzy. Still continued for a time, then forced my way slowly back, as I was getting nothing. Beetle's wings over door.

20' Pranayama.

7:15-35 Asana
7:35-55 Dharana
I don't know.
7:55-8:15 Harpocrates

Thought I could not finish this - very little mental concentration.
20' Pranayama, 10-20

Mar 17
A.M.
7:00-20 HALAHEL - Nix.

10:00-20 Asana

Get into this well for 5, 8, at rare intervals 10', then begins fight.

10:20-40 Dharana

Have started pool of still water. Been

getting myself rigid in spots - this helps.
Last 5' nix & I hear only argument Baron,
et al.

Joined the mob to fight about walls, etc.
Then all the things we had moved out of one
room we toted back again! Mess! Mess!!

P.M.
2-3

Type on record - I cannot settle myself to
anything else. All this confusion and noise
will help concentration, however, as I am
working through it at times.

MARBAS
Sense of deep green, then come to forest of
turpentine pines. Nothing else.

20' Pranayama, 10-20

8:35-55   Asana, water
Started out well - weakened.
8:55-9:15   Dharana, ditto
Harder, but hit a few times.
9:16-35   Harpocrates.
Stilled humming part of mind.

Have accomplished something! Let the fleas
bite - it matters not. Now, when I am indifferent to their walking'!. ----

29' Pranayama.

Mar 18
A.M.
5:55-6:25   HALAHEL - Nix; controlling of humming centre.

9:35-55   Asana
Fair, in places.
9:55-10:12   Dharana' Disk
Have discovered humming centre responsible
for ears partially "deaf", as sometimes occurs in biliousness, quinine taking. Got
hold here, but ware! Walk carefully, else
more attacks. Some connection here with sex?

20' Pranayama, 10:20
Diaphragm whimpering last 5'.

This work is telling on me. My appearance
is that of one "drawn through a knot-hole".
I wake during night, but sleep reasonably
soon afterward.

1921

P.M.	Typed on record - toted books.

Halahel, 20'
Concentration only.

10 or 15' Pranayama.

8:28-48	Asana
8:48-9:08	Dharana

Both peculiar quality; almost pressure from below, upwards.

9:10-30	Harpocrates.

A blank. But I am not to be caught napping & discouragement creep in. I understand any such attack.

20' Pranayama, 10-20

Mar 19
A.M.

4:50-5:05	Halahel.

I can't work; I feel like an empty cylinder, the engine gone.
I lie down a moment, get hold of something, rise and work till 5:25

No place to work. Painters in empty rooms & typing room packed to the gunwhales.

P.M.

8:30-50	Asana
8:50-9:10	Dharana

Getting humming centre into line at times.
In beginning linked up properly, as there seemed a certain ease & strength, coupled with dignity & power. Ended blank.

9:15-35	Harpocrates

Part of time something; most of time, nothing!

20' Pranayama.

Mar 20
A.M.

7:40-8:00	Attempt Halahel, but concentrate instead.

This humming centre is where false images arise, watched yesterday. That the part I have thought dissociated? And that caused Fee Wah to say "You let others use your brain?"
Is this reason for present lack of vision?
This spot busily occupied elsewhere while balance is trying to visualize.
Think this spot has some connection with sex, the weakest part of my armour, according to Fee Wah.

K2'

Go to Cefalu 9:15 with Lea to inspect paints.
Return 10:20. Start work 10:35. Tired from
hill climb, etc., lie down and work with now
famous centre. For 20' I listen with effort
to foot-steps, ticking of watch, voices - and
find this spot does not readily lend itself
to change; that had I the use of this only,
the overtones of voice would be lost. That is,
I take in   not
Think I am on track of a big change. This the
leak, this the chattering, the picture-forming,
the idle and false imaging centre; floating,
detached, from my conscious will.

P.M.   20' Marbas.
                Nobody home.

8:05-24   Asana
9:24-44   Dharana
                Body screeching.
8:45-9:05   Harpocrates.
                Dreadful! Got hold a trifle last 5'
              10' Pranayama.
                Throat tickling - coughing.

Mar 21
A.M.   Many happy returns of the day, Jane!

              No sleep early part of night. This A.M. so
                profound I did not hear the peasants!! Nor
                did I wake till 6:50 when Lea was around.
                No work, as painters are due at 7.

9:30   No painters.
9:40-10:00   Asana
10:00-19   Dharana
                Work not so loathsome - in fact, interesting
                at times.
10:20-40   Harpocrates.
                Don't know.
              Pranayama.
                Had to go to door three times. Good-night!

P.M.   Daubing around with paints, etc.

2:10-35   Marbas. Nix
              20' Pranayama, 10-20

Mar 22
A.M.   Birthday celebration, Lea and I. Pint of
                champagne, ½ capsule grass. Baron 7:30-9.
                I sat on his knee, he feels quite encouraged.
                Not sleeping by 10 I got me up and gathered

You can't hope
to do Dh until
your asana
is perfect.

Mar 1921

together from the four corners an opium out-
fit. Smoked 10:15-11. Nix.
We had some fun anyway.

10:07-25	Asana
10:25-44	Dharana

Wonder why body is easier at times.

10:45-11:05 Harpocrates

20' Pranayama.

P.M.   To Cefalu to see police, get hair cut, etc.
Fooled all round.

30' Disturbed concentration.
After this particular centre strenuously ex-
ercised, sleep well.

10' Pranayama, 10-20
3'   "   15-30

8:10-20	Asana

Missed fire all through.

8:20-40	Dharana

Did something.

8:41-9:09 Harpocrates
All off mentally.
3' Pranayama. Break.

So am I,

Am tired in upper spine and back of neck.

I wonder at what period of my past life I have
arrived in the digging up porcess. It is
years since I used to hum, over & over, "O,
the clanging bells of time", etc. The past
few days, digging deep, I have unearthed this,
long since forgotten, humming away.
Can I bring that song into conscious and so
rid myself? A leak, anyway.

Mar 23
A.M.
11:15   Have been to Cefalù about passport.
Tried vision this A.M., but there has been
strain somewhere and because of this shall
eliminate morning work and see if I can
rest strained part. Scenarios instead.

P.M.
8:18-38	Asana
9:38-58	Dharana
10:00-20	Harpocrates.

Almost I could become discouraged here. Never
get this

1921

7 Think I am on the trail of faculty of memory.

    6' Pranayama, 10:20
    Throat tickling.

Mar 24
A.M.
7:20-40   Halahel.
    Concentration only, a stilling of another
    buzzing part, farther up in my head.

    Restless during early part of night, then saw
    great opportunity to work on negative parts
    ∅ Did so, then slept soundly till morning.

9:58-10:18 Asana
10:18-33 Dharana
    Ignominious defeat. A cramp in sole of foot.
    So new a spot and so painful a drawing of
    toes and heel towards each other, I broke
    posture.
10:35-55 Harpocrates.
    Did I finally land here?
    20' Pranayama, 10:20

P.M.
8:30   Painter in and out everywhere.
    All day on scenario of Karma series.

8:37-55 Asana
8:55-0:13 Dharana
    So tired thought I could not do these, but did
    get hold of something.
9:15-35 Harpocrates.
    Last 10' a sitting still.
    7' Pranayama, 10-20

Mar.25
A.M.   Bad night. Lea up at 4:10 and off to Palermo.
    Painter thumping at 7 (after told 8) wakes me
    from troubled slumber.

9:11   Karma scenario, peddling from one room to
    another to accommodate painter.

    For 3 or 4 nights, coming from sleep of early
    night have noticed mind, xxxwhxx at work as
    in Dharana.

P.M.   More work on story, typing draft, etc.

7:40-8:10   Asana
8:10-30   Dharana
8:32-50   Harpocrates
            Think I get into Asana and Dharana better
            when I do strike nowadays, but strength
            seems all gone when H. reached.
            20' Pranayama, 10-20

            Last night's dream, of Hats!

            I had none. Discovered some one had presented
            me four, in four boxes; two small ones, which
            I did not see and two large ones, with wide
            brims. The first taken out of its box was
            a grey-green, soft, drooping brim, lacy edge,
            narrow band around crown, brought together in
            front by small rose - of pinkish-red with
            yellow showing through, I think. I was a
            trifle doubtful about this as I took it from
            its box, but found it most becoming and I was
            delighted.
            I am not sure of following sequence, "1" may
            have been "2"
            1. I heard my typewriter going and stepped to
            my door. (Should say the hats and I were by
            the pigeon-holes in Temple room.) Machine
            was being operated by invisible hands and I
            thought a message for me was being typed,
            message not finished I returned to hats.
            2. Took second box and drew out a most bi-
            zarre affair, black and white, of distinct
            lines and angles, trimming geometrical. Two
            tabs extended down on either side of face,
            from edge of brim against head, these were
            dotted. To my intense amazement, this too
            proved becoming.

Mar 26
A.M.   Last night I was shown the way, that on which
            to work, the result of proper work. Perfect
            repose in every part, no strain, a feeling
            of ease. I have been using up energy, in-
            stead of lack of it, equilibrating by cessa-
            tion, and am at the end of things. It may
            have been right for the time.

I now make the experiment, 10:05-25, and suc-
ceed. Myself a lotus on a motionless pool.
The central part of me coming to life - Being,
as distinguished from Mind?

4½' Pranayama.

P.M.   Am finding out these days why my lethargy, my
           lack of strength. I have been divorced from
           Being, I think; cut off from the vitalizing,
           main current.

15' Concentration in Asana.
20' Pranayama, 10-20
    Good, as will had to be active to keep going
    at all.

At intervals during day, Karma scenario.

6:00   I feel as though come to a full stop. A hav-
           ing finished and a waiting for the backward
           swing of the pendulum.

8:50-9:10 Asana
           Working easily and well.
9:10-20   Dharana
           Easy and good.
           In both of these the steady balancing as of
           delicately adjusted instruments.
9:20-40   Harpocrates.
           Nothing. I knew at 9:20 I was finished,
           but sat through Harpocrates. Does this do
           any good?
           10' Pranayama, 10:20
           Better than heaps of my 20' periods.

Mar 27
A.M.   Lea back from Palermo yesterday tells news
Moderne   about A.C. at Moderne? We try an experiment,
           she heroin, I opium.
        I get that A.C. did a worthwhile poem - a wish
           phantasy? And succeeded in smashing the
           vodka bottle. O for a picture of Lea's
           face when I told her!

Try vision, nothing.

10:20-40 Asana, Nix
10:40-11:0 Dharana
           Now think opium affects the delicate centres
           on which I have been working.
           5' Pranayama.

*Yes: but a healthy person
don't know about delicate
centres.*

P.M.   Letters to M.K.W., English Tea Rooms, Consul in Tunis.

15' Marbas. Nothing.
Can't visualize Talisman.

8:07-25   Asana
Part of me most conscious seemed to be on top of a crag reaching into the heavens. Equilibrating.

8:25-45   Dharana. Disk
Thelines on the disk are coming into play. The two straight across, for the last 3 or 4 days; this evening those joining centre from above. Steadying the mind and keeping it without a break.

8:46-0:05 Harpocrates.
Did something here with left lobe.

This about lobes is all balls

By far the greater part of my past work has been with left lobe. Freud has something to say about this.

20' Pranayama, 10:20

Mar 28
A.M.   15' Vision, nothing.

10:32-50 Asana
10:50-11:09 Dharana, disk
Disk now seems body, lines on it various faculties, all being drawn to a centre. Have not yet got definitely ascending lines.

11:12-28 Harpocrates
Nothing at all. Tried to free, used up energy, now tired in upper spine.

17' Pranayama.

P.M.   Work on Karma scenario.

You must analyse (& so destroy) all this sort of thing.

15' Vision.
Nothing, except possibly an indication of what lies within. A current of irritation deep within all day, now it pops to the surface over some picture suddenly thrown on the screen and I feel like beating Lea, the nearest to me, to get it out of my system.
I find this rather amusing, especially as it occurs to me I may do some whaling before

I am through, remembering my very intense desire last fall to wallop A.C.
Golly, I even see blood!

8:10-30   Asana
           Good
8:30-49   Dharana, disk
           Got upward lines, steadying astral? Last
           10' took in circle of disk with barrel-like
           cavity extending from left eye to back of
           head, this cavity expanding till taut.
           Had this experience in Harpocrates two even-
           ings ago, cavity descending from top of head,
           through left lobe, to same place in back of
           head, at that time.
8:50-9:08 Harpocrates.
           Heavens! Did something here, also!!.

           None of this work tiring. Am I acquiring
           equilibration? My aim.

           20' Pranayama, 10:20

Mar 29
A.M.   15' Vision.
           Equilibration only.

9:57-10:17 Asana
           Good
10:17-34   Dharana
10:35-53   Harpocrates.
           Last two simply impossible with all the
           racket. A holding self still only.

           I go to paint.

P.M.   Painted till 2:30
           Now for Lea's pants.

           More painting.

           With all this laborious painting, shall stop
           Yoga and smoke.

9:30-10:40 Smoke.
           Go after motto for Work. "It shall be".
           Later. Get 415 or 416 (think latter) for
           work with A.C.
           Later. No, it is 415.

Mar 30
P.M.   All day painting - book shelves and Circle.

Smoke at 8. A glorious wind blowing.

By the way, last evening, got a suspicious
note regarding Sullivan. What? He needs
watching, money enters into this suspicion.
Nor can I get a deep note with Sylvia. Perhaps all the joking about "Sylvia" at bottom
of this. But can she stand fleas and trees?

7

Mar 31

Abstract principle means more to me than concrete example. Peoples' approval, or lack
of it, carries little weight with me. Their
analysis of people and things interesting -
it shows what they are.

Painted from 8 to 6:50 P.M.

An inward peace and satisfaction these
two days.

From the way Russell has done the odd jobs
around here I am bound to say he either,
lacks intelligence,
lives in another world entirely (as I have
done for so long a time), or
does not care especially how a thing is done.
He works as the average Union workman - to
get the job over with and the pay envelope.

Centred entirely on magic?

Opium.
Had been wondering about loving in spite of
"evil", "dirt", etc., assuming one closed
one's eyes to that phase. I stepped into
that part of myself where, regarding ob-
jectively this very thing, it ceased to be.
One does not close one's eyes, anything ob-
jectionable ceases to be. All is love, no
room for aught else. This must be what I
term Spiritual Love.

Was getting something about copper qualities
not sufficient, there had to be the brass
also. Came out without real subject.
Copper beautiful, mellow, soft; brass, vital,
strident, strong.

Failed on another. Could not bring through,

then tried ushering in on sound.
  Something interfering. Sound was like a
  mosquito buzzing.

April 1
P.M.

All day, till 4, painting and varnishing.
  Hope to clean up to-morrow.

Opium.
  Came into consciousness saying "The Master
  Viencha" (so pronounced. Vienca?)
  Is there such?

April 2
A.M.

Peculiar night, waking every hour, then sleeping. Opium took form of sleep.

P.M.

Thought to be finished painting to-day, but
  no! More painting to-morrow. Did clean a
  heap of pots & brushes, however.

April 3   More painting, more scrubbing.

April 4   Smoked last night, the last I think, though I
  make no promises.
  Program for to-day, clean, clean, clean.

Yesterday I spoke to Howard between Adoration
  & tiffen.
To-day I say a sentence in English to Genesthai.

When I have time shall compare this with former breaks to see if opium has aught to do
  with it.

Go into Work in detail.

Odd jobs all day.

April 5   Good sleep. Last two opium nights cat naps
  only.

Genesthai getting Temple seats from wine room.
  Lea walks into wine room and says: "I think
  we would better dust those in here."
Two days ago, in dining room, Genesthai is
  troubled about the disposition of something.
  Lea says: "We want that (or them) put" so
  and so.
Of course, in both cases she may have been
  soliliquizing, so let her R.I.P.

Funny about the room proposition.

A short time ago the question of remaining
here or returning to Umbilicus entered my
thought. I debated and could not come to a
conclusion - it seemed both houses have ad-
vantages, both disadvantages.

Now comes A.C.'s letter "Sullivans in Jane's
old room." Lea says this means the typing
room. I thought Umbilicus, and I find my decision based on two reasons:

1. When I left for the Umbilicus I left so
completely I could not use the possessive about
anything in Abbey - nothing there ever had
been mine. And,

2. I found I had been hoping to be assigned
to peasants' room! Being isolated from everything and everybody.

April 6
A.M.
3:15

All night I toss, unable to sleep. Finally at
2:20 I seem to be in a bed where Hansi's now
stands, a hand is placed on right side of
head, I lying on left side. There is tremendous pressure in my head, upwards, and a
drawing up the spine. With this came a laps-
ing into unconsciousness. I did not know
whether it was sleep, so brought myself to
with great difficulty. Then deliberately
keep eyes open for some time. Finding myself still unsettled, I try Hanged Man. It
does not work. I sit up and for 15' work
in usual Asana. Not much accomplished.

4:00

I scribble some and am still wide awake.

P.M.

A.C. arrives.

April 7
A.M.

At Umbilicus, sleeping in boys' room. 'Nough
said. Awake since 5:30, after wakeful night.
And have discovered Lulu delightful: she
crowed and cackled from 6 to 7.

9:00

Did not enter that April 6, in Pentagram, got
what looked like a baking powder add I have
seen: a spoon heaped with powder. It may
have been a hand holding something. Indistinct because of bad mental state.

This morning in Pentagram (indistinct again

as I am still frightfully fatigued) what I
call the Saturn sigil with point below.
   During saying of Creed what seemed an eye
in a dark red field - i.e. an eye drawn by
hand, similar to one on A∴A∴ literature.
   No power; too tired I think.

(Should add, colours of yesterday and Saturn
 same as heretofore, blue, red and gold.)

April 8
A.M.

20' Asana
12' Dharana
   Difficult; thick. No calm serenity.

Pentagram.
   Started with sword and sceptre composed of ^Sunlight.
   At one time they were a brilliant ruby red,
   and maintained positions pictured. There
   were other symbols, other colours, but they
   came so fast I could not follow.

April 9
A.M.
5:45

Try Yoga. Unable.
15' Pranayama.

At Abbey all morning, discussing funds.
How much better in the essential matters of
life to be absolutely straightforward, frank,
simple! Suppose it does cost an effort? Is
not all Life an effort, and must not an occult-
ist face everything?

I saw ~~Pullerya~~ Fuller pictured in "Star in The
West". The face startled me, and I am curious.
Have I known him before? Should like to meet
him. A "female soul in a masculine body". Not a bit

Cabled M.K.W.

Letter to Marian Marshall re funds.

Some generalizations, in an attempt to understand myself, for I have never confronted me.
I feel and I don't feel. Somehow I managed a
long time ago to bottle up, to chain in the
cellar, or to muzzle, that part of me that
feels, and have lived - where? I don't really
know.

Yes, it is. He must. But
so many "occultists" being
thieves, I feel I must guard
the honour of the whole
Tradition by keeping my
hands more than clean -
antiseptic. So I am as
P.M.
sensitive as a gentleman
playing cards on a
'liner', who won't play
for money though he
does so in his club. I'm 'ashamed' even to sell my books, even
at less than the cost of production. To talk "business" at all is

to me a sort of immodesty. I feel like
a king obliged to pawn his watch, or like a
'pure' woman asking a friend for a loan, in agony
lest he should think
she was offering her
'virtue'. Equally, if the friend knew without doubt why
I want the money, I am ready to prostitute myself
not only shamelessly but proudly, glad to prove my
love for my Work
by love's greatest
martyrdom —
personal degradation!

I have had a talk with Genesthai regarding the
Tree of Life and I said "Good God!"
    As for the reason, I shall "hold back" as
Lea said I did. Thoughts are things, the fewer
the better. Some day I shall add a P.S. to
this entry.

P.M.
4:55 !

Test entry.
    For a long time I have felt Shummy will al-
ways be in my present life - if not in immedi-
ate personal contact, at least by post or other
means. I shall always know her whereabouts.
Genesthai once my son, and shall be again.

Have just realized that once I yielded myself
    completely. My terror in May, 1918, when,
    after many efforts attempting catalepsy, I
    collapsed, gave up all, and said: "I am afraid".

April 10
A.M.
5:30

Contending forces are playing hob with me these
days, and I understand. I must eliminate all
mental friction and loss of energy through need-
less use.

7:00   "Twilight of The Idols" since 5:30.

P.M.   Messing around with paint tubes, etc., all
            morning and till 3:30.

7:30   A long walk by the sea. To me there seems a
            something gone, like the stoppage of a current.
            There is something lacking that should be here?

Was a purse found containing 30,000 lire?
Night of the 8th I made a definite Invocation
and limited the time of its operation. Did I
mess things?
    And I am glad M.K. refused me her small money
when the Chiswick stock was purchased, for by
now it would have been used. We did without &
in our present extremity she may be able to stop
the gap till sufficient money shall have come in.
    Why this extremity, anyway? Have serious mis-
takes been made? Or is it that one or more of

Extremity due solely to
wise business decision
to 'carry on.'

I put in about 150,000. The expenses have been mostly investments. Our assets are now very large & only need to be realized. 100,000 will suffice for 2 years, as we have paid off mortgages on our property of various kinds

———————

Any such questions can be settled one by one as they arise. We are a Ship, and the Captain must be the sole authority for the sake of all alike. The Captain has the sole use of the sextant, despite the bosun's 'right' to hammer nails in with it, because the ship's safety depends

the people appealed to belong to this Circle and shall by this means be brought into it? Or, is it both? Or another reason entirely?

And why 100,000 for two years? In the last one, Shummy has contributed, roughly, 110,000. How much more has been added to this sum, and spent? Not very encouraging.

April 11
P.M.

Peculiar about Yoga. I cannot seem to do anything. I try.

"Twilight of The Idols" before turning in.

April 12
A.M.
12:50

I wake and the following thoughts occur to me.

Are we a Community, each contributing to the support of that Community; be it great or small, in labour or what, does not affect the question. Are we joint owners? If so, technically, is A.C. entitled to exclude anyone from the Abbey, say, in case anyone should desire to go there - except during a Cefalidian Working, for example? Is he entitled to set apart anything purchased with common funds for his own consumption, denying others? - Liquers, wines, etc., meaning less to me, I believe, than anyone else here I can raise this question. X

It might be well to face and settle, for future occasion - I should like to know at present - if this is:

An autocratic institution?
An A.A. organization & autocratic?
An A.C.   "   "   "
A Community?

Also, as yielding up our will, in case of dismissal who pays transportation expenses, etc. Or, should each one here protect himself by withholding sufficient to carry him to a place of safety, should occasion arise?

"Tristam Shandy" till I sleep.
(P.S. Which was 3)

6:25

"Body immortal as well as the soul." Why not? Can matter be destroyed?

By the bye, Nietzsche says "obedience humiliates".

× This is also the point (Real C&xx II 58) that we is entitled to have speaking to the has always been anxious to have on this restriction of it to the Captain.

Thus 666 reserves the absinthe, because it helps him to create scenarios whose sale will buy Ninette new clothes, and anyone else who drank it would mystifyeriely help the Establishment of the Law. 666 never drinks it merely as a pleasure. He is now writing this obvious stuff

10:25

Again I **try** Yoga. I knew I needed a rest, but it must be two weeks since I stopped! Well, I abide.

Meantime, I am attempting a study of myself. Of course, I have recognized from the beginning A.C. antagonized me - I antagonize him - the dislike is mutual. With an ocean between, it is different on my part. From one angle this is corking, an extremely wise arrangement. So, for the present, let it rest there.

I can pay both a compliment: strong - I almost said violent - natures are always offensive in some way. Though, as I understand mine is to be a public ministry, not the seclusion of an Abbey, say, it may be incumbent upon me at least to disguise the harshness.

In California none of this came up. The Ministry of Beauty, beauty of thought, beauty of action, beauty of surroundings, personal appearance and daily life, was a live thing with me. It was my rule of life, a rule which never proved irksome, never difficult. Here the reverse is the case. I want to be hateful, I want to irritate.

A good thing, too, when understood. Amen.

P.M.

A long walk up the hill, alone. Return and read aloud to Russell and Shummy "Androcles & The Lion." Always good for a laugh.

after painting and dictating simultaneously all day, & will probably work out a new scenario all night, helped by cocaine at the risk of his health and reason, all to get money to Establish the Law. He is not grumbling at his poverty-stricken surroundings, or regretting the $300,000 he has given to the Work, or withholding one drop of his blood from the 'Cup of BABALON.

over

and why shouldn't Hansi play with
any colours, and your typewriter, and Léa
grab Ninette's ripples from Lulu? SVVM CVIQVE

The antagonism between Metonith & 666
is the mask of their Love. She & he are alien
by race, caste, education, profession, &
temperament. But she doesn't get angry
because Ibsen bores her, or he because
the Esquimaux don't admire his poetry. But
he is furious because His Metonith has no
literary taste, & she because Her Breast
lacks the Quality of Bigness. But their
Love having made them one in soul will, little
by little, overrule these technical objections
as frivolous. Much has already been done,
& as Love works overtime every day, she will
soon conquer selfishness & suspicion, and he
accept American Barbarism as a Play of Wirth!

April 13
P.M.

Up Gibilmanna, and to Monastery, with Genesthai.
Left a few minutes after 10 - got back at 418.

April 14
P.M.2:15

A "Mithriac Ritual", handed me by Genesthai.
..."(a man, I say) presumes to worship Thee."
I have seen A.C. humble in Thoth (?) Invocation. No arrogance, of course, but why not the
Simplicity of Equality? A child may love, adore,
venerate a parent; yielding up its whole being.
But there can be no thought of presumption, hu-
mility.
I do not understand this.

April 15
A.M.

Letter to Bickie. Not "depressing" this time,
but clean crazy.

I ask Yi: "Shall I have my Retirement in May?"
And receive XIII.

It has occurred to me that I may know "Rich man
from The West", and I therefore ask Yi. And
receive that symbol which says "Oracles of The
Sun." This seemed to me at the time so far
away from my question I made no note of interpretation.
Wrong.

P.M.

Typed "The Bronze" and Timbuktu prospectus.

5:50

I feel like pulling out the cornerstone, watching the building topple over, and sitting down
in the midst of the ruins, the better to become
one with it. This takes me back to childhood,
when as pastime warm days was, to select a fine
pile of warm earth, sit in the midst of it and
pour the whole heap over head, shoulders and
body. Sounds demoralizing enough.

April 16
A.M.

In re my Abbey questions.
Perhaps I was too apprehensive about the future
of the Abbey, that time when more students should
be here and therefore greater danger of ship-
wreck if we are a Community. Autocracies live -
Communities, sooner or later, blow up violently
or disintegrate and fall apart.
The nature of the training necessary for the
Aspirant, it seems to me, precludes aught but
autocracy. My questions resulted from A.C.'s
calling us a "Community". The peoples of an

But a ship is a
community, though
autocratically governed

autocracy - Benevolent Despotism, let us say,
give their love - if necessary, their life,
their all, to the welfare and maintenance of
that Despotism. The peoples of a Community are
never satisfied. (Witness America!!!)

I find I rebel at "fixed principles", "fixed
standards". I am well aware they make associa-
tions easier, life more simple; for there would
not be all this misunderstanding, this useless
chatter. Yet, notwithstanding, why should there
not be diversity here, also?
Is this, too, "idiocy" on my part?

"You do not realize who I am."
How can I express what is in me? I do not use
Babalon in the Second Aethyr, but that which I
love, that which I venerate, that which per-
meates Me and has the power to fill me with ecstacy, has naught to do with output! It has
naught to do with caste, naught to do with education, naught to do with anything the world es-
teems. Were there none of these but instead a
toothless, senseless, gibbering imbecile, it
would be the same. It is all the Elements combined in one. It is All-Yielding, All-Absorbing.
It is Completion. What feeble language! When
shall I express Myself!!
Nor can I look out on any other than a level
of perfect equality: it is not possible. It is
not possible for it would not be worthy.
(And here I note that although, in the past,
I have used that term - "perfect equality" -
I never before felt it; there was always a barrier.)

Is aught degrading but thinking makes it so?
Does not herein lie one reason for the strength
of Japan? In California I have seen well train-
ed, well born, well educated Japanese, doing the
most menial work - for the time being, at least-
without loss of manhood, loss of dignity or self-
respect. When did they arrive at this Truth?

A dream which should have been entered yesterday.
I was in an unusually large square room in an
hotel. A.C. and Lea were there, seated at a
table in one corner, near a window, and to my
left, I seated on the foot of the bed, which

*I now understand the
marriage of a poor "white trash"
of The South too far idiots. On the
[illegible] is horrified & nauseated.*

explanation

position placed me toward centre of room. I
then found myself enveloped in a black lace
mantilla. It fell from over my head. With its
wearing I became coquettish, using my arms as a
dancer might in handling the lace. Evidently
no one in the room paid the slightest attention.
I found myself on a picturesque street in a
strange city, buildings close and compact, and
undoubtedly European. The street on which I
walked ascended, another street falling away
from it but leading in same direction, my street
above being balustraded. I then realized I was
to meet a youth of twenty, or thereabouts, he
waiting for me somewhere. Arriving at "A", I
seated myself at a small table of an outdoor
restaurant. The youth was seated, I knew just
below, though like a cat with a mouse I did not
see him at all. He became more and more impatient, and then a note was placed in my hand
which was sent by him. It was folded square,
I was quite conscious of this. I opened my hand
to read and found a bill of a 20 denomination.
This bill was about the size of a French 100
franc and of a similar blue & pink.
In this dream my name was Lola.

April 20
A.M. 7:45   Vision.
First a luminous light yellow-green. This for some
time: I paid no attention, having been looking out
the window and thinking it extension of physical
vision of some object. Then followed the other colours I have heretofore seen - reds, golds, blues;
the solid now one colour, the outline another. Do
not remember order of colour. Shape of symbol never
changed.

April 22
A.M.   Letter to Marian Marshall re Timbuktu.

April 26
12:30 p.m.

Please give
concrete
facts when
accusing people
your own note has just
the defects you observe
in others

"Talk not overmuch", but when one does talk,
for heaven's sake, let it be to the individual
involved or accused! One word then might eliminate all misunderstanding. (This includes
myself - too bad I have to so note).

Many things I noticed on my arrival at the
Abbey. One of them was this damnable beating
about the bush - no one able, it seemed to me
then, to say a straightforward "Yes" - "No".
Then after the occurrence, or lack of it, re-
criminations - "If you had done what I said",
etc. - an attempt to shift the responsibility.

This not yet weeded out.

April 28

I cannot see myself on the Rock: I doubt if I
shall go there at all. And I am wondering
if my "Retirement" will take place right here
in the Abbey? Of course, May, 1921, may not
be correct after all.

April 29

Karma No.1 mailed to M.K.W.

May 8
A.M.

During night mind was working on chess. One
move was given me which I knew to be quite
brilliant - it attacked the opposing King in
the King row, and in one move; it had a special
name. Neither move nor name stayed with me;
a Rook or Queen did the attacking, however.

Late morning dreamed I was in a large square
airy attic in a big building. I received a
rose bush from California, carefully pruned
for planting, the earth around the roots well
packed and still moist. I took it downstairs
to plant in the garden, over which my window
looked. Somewhere I met A.C. (I rather think
in the garden, though I did not seek him) and
showed him the bush. Blanche Sweet was also
in this building.

May 10
Afternoon.

This is the
great secret.
as a joke

I realize now how doing a thing without "Why?"
"Wherefore?" prepares one the sooner for the
service of the Gods - the elimination of the
personal. This has arisen in connection with
flagellation, recommended by A.C. after hear-
ing my dream of May 8th.

The peculiar thing about this, it seems to
me, is that something within desires this
experience, and immediately I say "Why!"

To start things going - if it will?
Curiosity - to have first hand experience?
Or, is it fundamental?

I have begun to suspect that I take pleasure
in inflicting pain by word -- No, I do not. I
do it, but not for pleasure: no, it is not my
Will. (I think I can trace this to my early
twenties. I shall see.)

Shall I discover an enjoyment of physical
pain?

8:45   Have read "Flagellation in France."

9:00   To widen my experience?
This wanting the experience is extremely subtle.
One can be restless for days then suddenly realize, say, a necessary ingredient is missing
from one's diet. But this is not of the physical. It seems too subtle to be of the astral.
Is it the soul? Has the mind aught to do with
it?

It's an obscure sexual complex

May 13
2:50 p.m. A cat nap.

Box oblong
About this size

I found myself seated at a low table, around
which sat several others. I shook a small box,
containing something which rattled like dice,
before each individual, whether in rotation or
alternating I do not remember. A.C. made some
remark I do not recall. I answered: "That is
what I am doing." While shaking think I was
saying "One, two, three, four, five, six, seven
eight", in time and tone as accompanying sketch.
I came to with a sense of mental whirling round
in opposite direction from hands of a clock,
although my body was seated at a table.

May 14
10:30

The Pure Fool has no objective.
That must be correct, yet how about Will?
Will says: "Travel from A to M". Therefore M
is an objective and one's destiny is not accomplished unless one achieve M. Make this dual-
ity one - how?

Indeed, how?

This also takes me back to a discussion with Lea,
about "watching each steap".

It strikes me Russell works with lust of result. He climbs the rock, he takes grass, to
get to the top, the quicker he gets there the
better. Would not the Fool forget about the
top? Would not he see all the detail en route,
indifferent as to whether he achieved the top
in a day, a month, a year? I see that the use
of the word "watch" might easily mislead one as
to my meaning - it was not a happy selection.

May 15
A.M.

Yes; but you must pass that point, it's an Ordeal

I have got to what for me is a demoralizing point, the challenging of everything I think or do to detect lust of result. Everything, from one angle is just that thing - aspiration for union, the preparation for the Work assigned one.
    I am in Midwinter's shoes.

P.M.

9 drop of grass.
Two flashes of unadorned Desire - not pretty.
Money just clearing water front of U.S. - perhaps one day out.
Have discovered that a certain drawing back of the upper lip which heretofore has always repelled me, really attracts - perhaps I should say, I found myself in harmony with it.

Probably

May 17

Shall I find the voluptuary in myself, that which is best illustrated by the cat luxuriating in warmth and laxily stretching itself in a physical ecstacy?

May 18
P.M.
4:20

Another instance of losing a proper focus through haste? Getting one thing & assuming that one thing to be all? I have said; "I cannot see myself on the rock". Should I have said: "I cannot see myself in the little house at which A.C. & I looked"? (I stick to the former. May 29.J.W.)
    Just returned from a climb to High Boy with Genesthai & on the opposite side from our abode, directly over the water, in the Temple of Jupiter, is a house with roof intact, without doors or windows, put up by the Italian government during the war, no doubt, as it is modern.

May 19
P.M.
6:00

Good

I have been thinking of it a good deal.

May 14 I was given distinctly: "The Pure Fool has no objective." For days I have been restive, impatient, chafing at the bit. I have realized Desire must be at the root of it, the fact that it was for Understanding, power, to go ahead and achieve, to help out in the present dilemma, makes no difference. To-day, not being dressed warmly enough coming from the bath, I chilled, went to bed and all afternoon lay in a fever. At the supper hour I heard A.C.'s voice: "I have been thinking of Jane's retirement; it seems impossible." This broke me down. I lay still for some time

the tears rolling down my cheeks, my pride was
gradually eliminated, and I finally said: "Fee
Wah, Elder Brother, Gods, take me as I am; purge
me." I found myself high up on a rounded hill.
Straight ahead, some distance away and seen over
the tops of trees growing below the curve of the
hill, lay the sea, high mountains at either side
of it, though the left line of ridges filled more
of the picture, than the right frame of the sea
being a tall, spire-like rock. The path on which
I stood, though clearly enough defined, was completely covered with dead grass. To my left, out-
lining the path, dead briers of the berry variety,
growing a trifle higher than the knee. The ground
rolling up and back of them covered with dead
grass.Then to my right appeared Elder Brother (?),
the path earth back of him falling directly into
a ravine. We stood in the sunlight. All Desire
by this time had dropped from me. I felt for this
being a great. love and I yearned earnestly to merge
my being in his - to lose myself. But I did not.
I rested against him till thoroughly imbued with
the "stooping starlight", and then went on alone;
for one second, when realizing I was alone, a tim-
orous feeling, which I was able to conquer. I
then passed on a few yards and began the descent
on the path, slightly curving to the left and now
closed in by a pine forest, so that the path was
lost in darkness. I then realized Elder Brother
was clothed in black.

I next found myself on the floor of the valley
below the path where I first stood. I found here
dead vegetation growing low on the ground, the
valley narrow like a hall almost, while all round
the cliffs rising high. And I said: "My way the
valley, not the peaks." And I went forward, simply and without aim, in the direction of the sea,
though I saw no distance ahead.

(I did the same thing May, 1918, when, having
been led up on a high mountain, I saw before me
a scene of ravishing beauty - a basin, the sun
shining through silvery mists lying below and
bringing into view an exquisitely beautiful land-
scape. I gazed, intoxicated, then turned my back
and said: "I choose the valley", which lay dark
and drear in front of me, and descended into it.)

    L.V.Jefferson, through sister's letter dated

April 28: "Jane is marking time; will shortly leave there - I get Burma: a tall man in belted robe, double turban effect, standing in belt of sunlight, back to me. Jane comes up behind. After coming into sunshine she becomes very happy - the first time since leaving California, and starts out as though she had a definite aim, springy-footed, her whole attitude expressing eager joy in mission. There is much growth, but not the tangled untrodden jungle. Will not return to the United States under two years."

I cannot see a G.M.R. I had the impression as I stood on the path first and alone, that the plan outlined was too much - I had not the strength? It was then I said: "Take me as I am", etc.

Or is it not the Plan? A Tarot divination by Genesthai says it is not my will nor the will of the Lords of the Aeon.

G. can't do Taro yet

May 21
A.M.

All day yesterday I was free from any Desire - things looked different. I offered to take over the washing of Lulu's diapers, etc., and meant it. Two days ago I could not have done this - easily. This brings me to the Christian Science way - their expression being: "There is no need to give up anything, or worry about error: you outgrow things." I have noticed this same thing take place with me - the dropping away, the sloughing off, without thought aimed in that particular direction.

May 23
A.M.

Last night before sleeping I practised 10' concentration, without an object on which to focus. When relaxing I found the right lobe was the field of my activity!

May 24
P.M.

I made the statement: "I never tire so long as I am interested." I now eat crow! I was tired today - all day; I felt wobbly in my back because of climbing up and down from tables & chairs and pulling chairs up after me. Yet I know I am interested in painting that wall. I go back to my stage days. One stands before an audience, alert, animated, because one is interested in doing the

thing, when off the set one collapses in the
arms of a helper or physician, or curls up in a
knot on a nearby trunk, insensible to everything
& everybody, till across the brain flashes the
cue. Yet the interest is there.

May 25
A.M.
All night in a mood I could not analyze - I can
not even name it. Irritation is too light a
word, yet it was not anger. We say a person is
"moody". What do we mean?
    Also came, during the night an argument that
brought forth without thought - "would engraft"
That word "engraft" leaped vividly into my mind
and obliterated all else. It takes me back -
but if one can engraft one can chop off! At
present I cannot accept the latter.

May 26
5:10 A.M. 25' Pranayama.

May 27
4:28 "A;M 20' Pranayama.

Typed A.C.'s poetical version of the Yi. This
morning before returning the book, I open the
map which shows the hexagrams placed in a cirle.
I run my finger around, with closed eyes, and
select one. Ming I. XXXVI.

P.M.
For the first in a long, long time, I turned consciously, gratefully and with love toward my
Unseen Helpers, and there seemed, at a great dis-
    tance away, a shimmering of vermillion and green-
gold.

These are the
Hierophant's colours.

May 28
6:10 A.M. 20' Pranayama.

May 29
A.M.
10' Pranayama.

Strange. On the edge of sleep last night, I was
conscious of rich blues and I felt love permeate
me and I exclaimed "Aiwaz". Hadit, Nuith, Aiwaz,
et al, have been but names to me. Melchisedeck,
Amoun - no; they have life.

A far away state during the night, in which I

found myself pregnant of two children. They lay
side by side, not one above the other as I understand is the usual way with twins. These two
symbolic of a spiritual (?) impregnation of two
branches of work? of two powers?
   (Does this connect up with the "boy and a girl",
I wonder?)

P.M. A Tarot divination for me by Frater Genesthai,
and copied from his notes.

1. Jane must get the number of her Magical
name, so that when in the operation she knocks
she will get the spirits which are harmonious
to her number.
2. Done. Her number is 516 = 12

Ace of Pantacles.
Ace of Swords Five of Cups
The Fool   Nine of Wands
Eight of Wands   The Sun.

Significator - Material; represents a Hé final
  course.
Positive. If she can overcome her parsimonity
in regard to loss in pleasure, she will find
herself with great strength. If she, then, takes
the path of the Moon she will find illusion. If
she aspires directly to the Moon, she will find
herself Lord of the Fire of the World, the Sun.
Contra. If she continue to be afraid of loss
in pleasure she will find herself immediately
as the root of the all-wandering air. But it
is Tetragrammaton spelt backwards, going from ה
to י. She will find that the force already invoked in her will carry her to Aleph which equals
Zero. But there is a gap between Aleph and the
Fool but for the fact that the Ace of Swords is
the root of air, which is Aleph. But she cannot
stay there long enough to accomplish her will,
in which case she will go right back again to
loss in pleasure. On the left, two steps take
her to 8 of Wands; on the right, one step takes
her to 9 of Wands.
   From Mars in Virgo she passes to Moon in Sagittarius. She goes from Yod to Samech and from
a masculine to a feminine principle - 10 (Virgo)
to 60 (Sagittarius) would be from (from I to IN)
a concealed force to an operation of the Gnosis.

From 5 (ה) to 9 (ט) is from taking the active part in that operation to taking the feminine part. But 10 + 9 = 10 = XIX, the Sun; and 60 + 5 = 65 אדנ׳ the Holy Guardian Angel. In which case she will find herself with great strength. If that strength be used to aspire directly to the Moon, not directly in the path of the Moon, she will find herself at the Sun. Otherwise she will be caught in the path of the Moon.

She does not want to get caught in the math of the poon, because she is in the math of the Nith. ר׳ר = 451. Mathonith = the 441st of the 451 = the Truth of the Sleep of Siloam (שׁ׳ל׳אח) it is the Live Coal in the Abyss; it is the Demon which balances the Essence of Man.

She finds herself then in the Sun's ray, in the path of the Sun in the letter Samech; i.e. she is in Resh and Samech at the same time. If she allows the gravitation of the Moon to draw her backwards she will fall into Yesod. The is the Yesod of Malkuth, etc. It is the Tree of Life in Malkuth. If she grasps firmly with her right hand the letter Samech, she will, by the aid of the letter Resh, of the Sun itself, reach Him, unite with Him, and become the Lord of the Fire of the World.

Samech is Sagittarius, aspiration to the Holy Guardian Angel. Its number is 200 (20 x 10). Samech is only 6 x 10. But (20 + 6), x26 x 10 = 260, which is the I.N.R. of I.N.R.I. Samech Resh is one's true will accepted, and Resh Samech is one's true will declined.

By the fact of the angle between the path of Samech and Resh, the form of attainment should be of the expansive, opening up, or feminine order, but it must be contained within the left-hand upper quarter of the tablet of air. But she has started out she-has-started-out from the tablet of earth. Consequently she will be weighed down and not up. She will find herself united with the One who represents the name she really heard, but, on account of the Moon, heard and spoken wrong. But she will be merely uniting with that name on the plane of earth, and it will be with ד׳ח׳ט not with the ס׳שׁ׳ה aspect.

Appendix.
This is a direct answer to her question, no matter how it was put, if it had anything to do with Aiwaz. It simply shows what relation should be made between her and Aiwaz. So we see she

[handwritten in left margin:] True; the math of the poon is a terribly seductive snare.

gets exactly 516 by 93, by interpreting the symbols she obtains, which exactly represent the
numbers she invoked.

Divination is then simply solving an equation;
x, the unknown answer, is equal to y, the question. By solving the first half we have solved
the other half (Liber Legis commands this), because the Universe is in equilibrium. But one
doesn't get O = O; one gets O = X, for there is an
inversion. But suppose one start - in solving
both sides at once. One whirls the left-hand
cube to the right and the right-hand cube to the
left, and they will each be doubled - making
Three-in-One. How many times one has to whirl
the cubes round depends on how much they are
twisted. One might find one'self when one stopped
at the same point of view as one had before, but
it would be the point of view of the Three-in-One,
which considers equations in their general as-
pects, rather than in their particular. He is
trying to find another equation to represent the
former equation (a synthesis of it). He finds it;
and it is O = O.

This is the most unintelligible
drivel I have read for a long
time.

It is wholly undesirable to
confer with flesh & blood.
There is only one thing to do; to
stick to your Work, without lust
of result.

May 31
P.M.
10:30
	Read Book of the Law and that portion of Temple of Solomon the King in No.X. Dozed and came to with these marvelous words of wisdom referring to an Initiation!
	  "He sewed up" (a pig) ::.......
	  "And out it ran again,
	  Poor old man!"

11:30	My first glimpse of Love for the Collegium ad Spiritum Sanctum at Cefalu. Heretofore reason only has acclaimed it.
11:40	"Why?", "Wherefore?" constitutes duality. Doing a thing qithout question eliminates it.
11:54	Bab has been here, radiantly happy. Yet there is something ominous about this - a something that almost makes me fearful.
June 1 A.M. 12:10	I lay quiet for a time, then "Bab" returned. Not instantly did I recognize the imposter, but I did realize that I was not one with this one ፀ I remained unmoved; then came gleaming teeth. It seemed something animal-man, head rounded at top like that of a cat. I did not see the eyes. I was as self-possessed as I would have been with Hansi. On my recognition and lack of fear it disappeared.
P.M.	Smoked opium this evening at Horsel; to my room at 10:15.
Later	Textla. The meaning of this word fully describ ed to me, yet I can recall the name only. Also I was shown the "strength, force, and vigour" of the direct line from the individual to God - no intermediaries.
June 2 A.M.	Waked up with headache, which soon disappeared, though there was a return of it for a moment while bathing.
June 4 A.M.	I now see for myself the necessity of releasing body, mind, to the uses of the Will, without any restrictions.

P.M.   The Key of the Mysteries. The "Spirit of Char-
        ity" is a real, a live thing: I grasp that. To
        make it a part of one's life!

        Attract - do not pursue.

        "Abandoned themselves to the delirium of a pas-
        sion."

June 6
A.M.   Quite without conscious thought on my part a
        link was established with Ra Hoor Khuit - the
        name has taken on a degree of life.
          This sort of thing has happened to me a number
        of times, and I wonder which is the better plan?
        To keep the aspiration true and let the rose un-
        fold naturally, petal by petal? Or, by a system
        of willed exercises, open up to the core one side
        of the rose?

P.M.   One may say the former, but occasion may demand
I seem to be climbing the latter - in which case it would be the better.
one side myself

        This afternoon I tried to get hold of the Spirit
        of Truth. I was in the typing room on the floor,
        A.C. on the couch, Lea typing. Could I have got *aught*
        alone? I must reach this.

11:50   A long talk from A.C. regarding my Retirement -
        at the Caldura.

June 7
P.M.
11:30   Worked for Spirit of Truth - got hold of something
        but what?

11:45   Does a pinkish-lavendar mean aught?
        A little later a brilliant green.
        Afterwards a brilliant blue.

June 8
3 A.M. Find myself still revolving round the Spirit of
        Truth, though not so deeply as last night. I
        have been wakeful all this time.

8:45   Read Key to Mysteries till 4, then fitful sleep
        till now.

P.M.

(1)

lines black

No bathing - painted most of the day, then at 4:30 started opium. No appreciable effects except a wonderful, luminous ruby red outlined in black, the line of black against the red soft though distinct. A black line also passed through the centre of the body of red.

10:00

My thoughts passed to Del Moral, a handsome Portox Rican boy, an admirer when I was in the teens. He spoke but little English, I no Spanish, yet we passed a couple of hours together almost in silence. The turn of a hand, the use of a handkerchief, the elevation of an eyebrow of vast import: the slight turn of a foot a poem. Is this lost as one gets older? There must be mental stimulus or contact of bodies to keep two people interested. The former is called "calf love", but I am wondering if much has not been lost by being unable to take so keen a delight in watching bodily play.

Many fleeting pictures, and I am wondering if the painting of the walls does not cause these. There was one very quick flash in which a fox took the place of Lea. I found this amusing - it should have been a "monkey"!

11:35

There has been a very strong Ra Hoor Khuit vibration. Shall I next find Nuith and Hadit mean life to me? All these momths I have stood apart. I read the Book of the Law as I might study a mathematical problem - coldly. In the past two weeks two names have taken on life - I have got a significance of one or two statements.

June 9
A.M.

I have been thinking of the R.H.K. vibration. Some pictures one sees and stands apart from. Others one sees and there seems to be a link - an electric light wire, say.
Again there is a decided response - such as last night - without the picture.--(What is the colour? There must be one.)
All vibration has colour and sound also. The musician gets the harmonies of sound; the artist, the colours; the poet, the rhythm of words - the great poet, all three. Is this why poetry is the greater art?

P.M. I have felt unusually well all day. About four
o'clock I lay down and consciously applied "I
am the strength, force, vigour". Call down fire
from heaven? Why not strength when one has need?
A reservoir one can always tap, I am sure, when
one knows how.

June 10
A.M. I experience the old feeling of aloofness -
what seems at times contempt - for Aiwaz this
morning. The fact that the wire has vibrated,
and in what seemed a satisfactory manner - has
made no difference, apparently. I feel that I
could with safety measure swords.

June 11
10:42 A.M. I walk to the Horsel - nobody astir. So I return. Passing the mill I suddenly realize the
meaning of an entry of June 1, "no intermedia-
ries". It stirs me so I all but roar aloud in
laughter! An aspirant for probation to A..A.. ,
while ~~admirimg~~ admiring and being helped, guid-
ed, strengthened by Beast, does not set him up
for worship as does a Catholic the Christ, the
Virgin. So with Aiwaz, Ra Hoor Khuit, et al.
"You must go to God not to me" said Fee Wah.
So would say also Ra Hoor Khuit. There is a
strange happiness and exhiliration in this
knowledge.

Later. I also realize how much better prepared I am
for the Retirement at this time. One month ago
it would have been an intensely personal thing.
A seems a year since then, so much has this personal attitude dropped away from me.

June 13
A.M. Only a free man knows how to love. In California I killed God. I think now I have them all
killed!

I go into Retirement to-day.

The 169 Adorations.

I do not know where this goes in the story. Perhaps a good strong pair of eyes can locate the Ritual. But some of the diaries were deet royed when they were sent to England. I do not recall what preceded this Work, but I do remember that I lay in bed at evening, propped up, holxinv a copy of Equinox III
. From this Vol I chanted the entire 169 Adorations aloud, adding in addition another half of these Adorations every night. I do not recall how many evenings I performed the Ritual, but I knew it was working.

One evening 666 told me to enter the Circle and perform the Pentagram. And possibly the Collects from The Mass. When walking around the Circle, pronouncing these at inervals I was flung to the floor; my spectacles sliding along the tiles without breaking, myself then rising and continuing the Collects till finoshed. I then went to my room for the night.

To learn the next morning that it was the first considerable movement of Kundalini. The former activity being at this moment beyond my memroy, This occasion was the appearance of the Green and the Red.

(Keep this sheet unused. There was intense activity in London.
Speak of this greater activity???)

A. C's 2 trees wherever
he located himself.

Cdfalu. Pn an Oath of Silence. Thr food arrangement.

I had a primus stove which I used for my morning needs.. The noon meal was brought from the Abbey by Genesthai, a then student: with the greeting: "Do what thou wilt shall be the whole of the Law!". My response: "Love is the law, love under will." The same with the evening meal. No other speech. Remember that Oath of Silence.'

My exercise between meditations was taken in the Mai Meditarrean, nude. Also by slowly dropping off rocks - to yield up Egos, and so on.

But I am anticipating the beginning!

Aleister had a splendid tent, used by him on his mountain trips heavy canvas, waxed. The pole containers stitched onto the outside. The same material for the bittom of the tent; which furnished a piece of the same canvas to keep water out of the tent. One had to step up and over into the tent. Also tie the tent shut if it rained. Waterproof all around.

Genesthai stationed the tent on the beach. The proper words were dpoken. All went back to the Abbey, while I retired on my palette - afrwe ny rituals to a sound sleep. I waked in the morning to a strange motion; looked around and found mtself floating, the tent poles keeping me from going out to sea somewhere - possibly!

A.C. and Genesthai had come to the top of the ~~top of the~~ trail to see how I fared; and immediately came down to save the satgo. This broke my 31-day Retirement. Genesthai and I talked! Helped one another to perch.

Russell then helped to put me up on rocks. A roaring storm that night chased me - alone - on a small hillside. Here I had no hekp whatsoever from anyone. So here I stayed doing my own tent-work, on the above hill-side. Which A.C. said was the proper thing.

Retirement. 13 ½   Cefalu.

At free times during the day I carried stones and rocks to give me a level floor for the tent and uts interior for practises. I felt like an Egyptian working on a pyramid.

I attracted some attention -- a few stones came through the air, one cutting thw. tent and landing on my head ½ without more than a sore spot.

The Italians thoought I had "The Pest" and by some eans or other I was to be sent elsewhere.

The police investigated - I went on with my meditations. Toward the end, sitting in boiling oil described somewhat of it. As the Princess who sat on pilwi up mattresses hoping to miss a wee small pea at the bottom of the pile. The two spots remained f r some time, but the ache of asana left the ankles and legs quickly.

Before leaving my camp I discovered my rigid body slowly leaning over and over, until I lay on the floor on my side remaining in my asana.

The night of my return to the Abbey 666, and all members robed -- with 666 be-medalled and robed magnificantly. He placed me witx standing with Sword on the oute r rim of "The Circle". I met Mary Butts, an English writer then at the Abbet. Also her companion one Cecil Maitland. I remember that for some time The tope of my head.felt ....   Mary had had an unusual psychology. When she didn't want to do a something A.C. designated she became feverish and had to lie down (for instance: Serving coffee for breakfast for the group.) I also went into a fever when I feared my Retirement might be withheld.

    (I go into Retirement June 13, 1921)

    The 169 Adorations & tneir result. Put in where suitable --
       no diary for these dates.

The Bornless One first; The Adorations second

1922.

Jan. 8. I have for several days been typing A.C's Gnostic Records, and it now occurs to me to start what may turn out to be one of my own. Some days past I felt the need of more strength, and decided to investigate this method of securing it.

But I shall first note here some experiences of the past two months.

While typing Book 4, Part III, Nov. 12/21, ~~suddenly~~ the sentence "the kisses of the stars rain hard upon thy body" leaps out of the page. It inflames me slightly, + I go to work! Stumbling about along these lines, using Nuit, Stars. +c., my imagination finally pictures phallus of mine Angel in the anus, + I instantly sensed the spiritual, and received the spiritual significance of sodomy.

Nov. 14, working along these same lines—
i.e., lying on my back, relaxed, and al-
lowing Sexual Sensation to flow through
me, which it did without (so it seemed)
any assistance on my part) — the Phallus
of my Angel seemed to fill my entire
body and head. In some part of my being, I know not where, there was orgasm,
intense. After a short interval again
there was a similar internal orgasm,
this time caused by a feeling (?) that I
was the Phallus of mine Angel. No;
that I was the skin surrounding it
+ was therefore a part of his body.

Dec. 31. "All day I have been conscious
of Sex force. Now, 9.30 p.m., I have just
had a Realization of the Holiness and
Sublimity of my work along these lines."
With this a consciousness of Soul touching

Soul (shall I say) in this way that is impossible to obtain in any other way.

Therefore with this knowledge and that derived from the Records, I started a definitely planned campaign. So Jan. 5, feeling Sex force automatically flowing through me, I invoked Pan, and started work. As I wish to gain mental control it seems best to abandon imagination & therefore I titillated the anus — as I wish to rouse it. And also there is the "Spiritual significance of sodomy". I stopped just before orgasm & consciously threw all this energy into reserve force. This seemed not only beneficial at the time, but there was a feeling of well-being all next day.

Jan. 7, on retiring, again was sensation coursing through me. Again I invoked

Pan, and then went to work as before mentioned. I also asked guidance in the matter. This time I dipped into mental concentration on any object (Energy) I held it well for a time, I think; then presume I tired. This time orgasm started, but I managed to stop it. My long training in the control of "Dreams" is bearing fruit!

I then felt a desire to take heroin, which I did, asking for a message as to whether my work was correct. Under heroin strength seemed to flow up my spine & into the head. After a time a something from a long distance away, ~~seemed~~ & descended ~~&~~ into my head. There was a feeling of expansion and relaxation..

It has just occurred to me that this

may be the "definite work shortly" of Dec. 26, and the "nearing of the Gate of Initiation" of Dec. 31, mentioned by me in my other Record as "impressions" or "intuitions" of something about to take place.

To date there is a feeling of better concentration all round.

Perhaps I should add that I have at no time undertaken work along these lines unless there has been an "automatic" Set Sensation — I have not consciously called it up.

An XVII O in ℔. All this is very good; but I repeat the old warnings against being satisfied with subjective sensations however intense & convincing they may appear.

But in this instance there is confirmation. Yesterday, in ignorance of what Soror ELTAI was doing, I spontaneously remarked that her eyes were unusually brilliant, her complexion clearer than I had ever seen it before, her aura most singularly pure and radiant. There is thus independent evidence of the correspondence between the observed result and that which is theoretically to be expected from the operations performed. I am therefore ready to admit that her work has been successful; for there is no other explanation, the rest of her conditions (weather, diet, her mental + moral situation etc) being unfavourable to her well-being.

I recommend the employment of a material assistant such that emotional distractions are unlikely to disturb the sacramental concentration. The proper formation and consummation of the Eucharist requires careful attention. The Objects of the Working must be chosen systematically. My own Record has all the faults of Pioneer-work: it contains much to avoid. There must be proper tabulation of the Experiments, and strictly scientific observation. Sentimentality, sexual or spiritual, must be sternly suppressed. Compliance with these conventions should assure a success far greater than I have myself attained. The Beast 666.

Jan. 9.
Very tired when I went to bed at seven o'clock + fell asleep. Waked at nine and felt an urge to work. Invoked Pan.
Found my mind distracted between

"Guidance" + "Energy". The former now
out: concentration flowed from, or was
centered in centre at base of brain; it then
shifted to centre between shoulders. After
this came a focussing on Energy.

No orgasm, of course!

Jan 11. This cleared + strengthened what?
Something was benefited, but the physical
felt the strain, as my back distressed me
all of the tenth.

———————

Jan. 13. 10. p. m.
Sex force flowing in the afternoon, I
therefore planned work for this evening.
Composed myself at eight o'clock with 2
doses of heroin, as my mind was hopping
about. Did not know what God I wished to
invoke, so repeated "Nuit, Hadit, Ra-Hoor-
Khuit" and asked for guidance. This
time I lay quite still, my hands folded
across my chest (my usual attitude,

by the way, when concentrating after retiring)
The mind took up accustomed routes; — all
wrong: it seemed there was to be something different. Several times there was a
starting + each time objective consciousness leaped in. After a time my whole
being radiated Love toward one who
seemed to be in my room, through there
was no hint as to who or what was
there.

Should enter here that I did not
want to work at all + had to overcome
considerable opposition.

An opportunity missed? Or, was it
because I felt on a brink + could not
plunge over?

Think I may have spoiled the whole
plan by smoking a cigarette, which I did
to wake myself thoroughly — there was a
drowsy feeling after a time. No work after smoking.

Jan. 14 P.M.

Thought to continue last night's work, but all ~~seemed~~ was dull. My mind took up "Nama Shivaya Namaha Aum", & instantly my whole being came to life! But I did no work along IX° lines.

Phyllis'

1922

Sept.4 Been through several days of spiritual depression.
To-day is gorgeous; sunshine, cool & delightful
wind. I feel like kicking up my heels and hoofing
it toward Gibilmanna. O, for a tramp with a con-
genial companion. Think Bickie's letter to A.C.-
helped boost my spirits. It was a pleasure to
hear from her again.

p.m. Howard and I up Gibilmanna road to the 'Summit'.
Blackberries, grapes & many figgerinis (given us)
on the way. He tired at intervals going up - coming down frisky as a young goat. We stole a big
bunch of grapes coming home.(Beastly things they
were too, without flavour.)

Sept.6 O Nuit, continuous one of Heaven, I see somewhat
of my stupidity, error & selfishness with regard to
Thy servant Therion. I understand more of His suffering, more of His labour, more of His passion;
His knowledge & wisdom. And I am now willing to
learn of Him. Yet, am I willing to give myself
utterly to Him? I think I shall still question.
I know not where I am; but this I do know: that
I wish to be more kind to Therion, more helpful,
more compassionate.

Sept.7 Up to Gibilmanna, leaving about ½ after ten, returning about six. Fiesta there, and the devout
making a pilgrimage to the Madonna, some women
with hair streaming, walking in stocking feet,
and approaching the shrine in the church on their
knees.

Sept.8 These long walks are not for me at present. The
trip with Howie wearied me exceedingly. Yesterday's trip left me so exhausted & aching I could
not sleep. Took a sedative. Again I got the
'Shot Drill', but I must go far beyond that, for
I am to have the Understanding of the God-purpose
in Life.
Bozella - Bozell - Bosell? Some connection with
the Moon.

p.m. A short nap. A.C. said "Ninette thinks Netzach
is upset by Hod." Does this refer to my present
condition? All bodily force concentrated in my
head?

Sept.9 Following out above, I kept my mind out of things
to-day; no reading, no thinking. Sewed nearly all
day and forced emotional nature to the fore. No
head trouble all day.

Sept.19 8-10:25.p.m. Straight ahead work of a nature never before undertaken. I know not how to describe it. Getting the steel frame of the building cleared of all plaster, trim windows, etc. might do. The plaster, etc. a rather sweet sensation, quite intense at times. The steel, stripped, without sensation; an impersonal thing. This stripping in all centres of my being. After, this work continued at intervals, and there came an impression that s. would feed and renew something used up in this work. Took 2 sniffs about 11:30 and worked at intervals till after two. Slept till 6:30.

p.m.   Slept two hours.

This a.m. a few words with Ninette at the table occasioned by table manners of the boys. She says I never finish what I start, referring to this matter and Hansi carrying water mornings. The ltter job I never took on, only stepping in a few mornings when she had no control of him. About the table - I wonder? It does seem to me that a meal does not go by that I do not speak. Difficult, not only because the constant work is wearisome, but because Ninette sometimes acts grouchy when I address Howie. His & Lulu's manners are common. (Rather early to judge Lulu, however.) Hansi has an innate grace which shows at times. His outer manners are imitations of the peasants; i.e. he objects to cutting his spaghetti and wants to suck in the long strings. He spreads his legs & spits, and in other ways imitates the peasants.

Sept.12 Still no news from London (2 weeks) & I am horribly distressed about Lea. A bit of peevishness, too, because we are kept in uncertainty about her.

p.m.   What fatality is about Ninette these days? Yesterday two big bottles of perfume smashed in her room; this morning at breakfast a glass containing cream slipped through her fingers & broke; at the above time (about) the big black Masque fell with a crash, breaking off the jaw and jarring loose bits of the brown plaster covering the face. She had replaced it on the nail a few moments previously, after looking at the back of it to see of what it was made, and telling me that Helen thought it looked liked me. But perhaps my looking at it caused it to fall?! After she left the room I remained, comparing it feature by feature with my

face. It fell with a crash while I was so looking!
Maybe it objected.

Sept.13 A weary spirit this a.m. Or is it the spirit?
Awake a long time last night. At times I cannot
keep away depression caused by sleeplessness.
Tired all morning in spine - Anahata centre?

Sept.14 Two soldiers called, inquiring when A.C. would be
back.
For the first time in my life I am feeling contempt for humanity. I have often wondered how one
who Understood, who had the Light, could feel contempt, if all is in God and of God.
Just spoke to Ninette about this 'contempt'. S
She says "for the individual". So I will add "for
the stupidity of the individual", and eliminate
'humanity'.
I think there is something back of the London
silence. Anyhow, I shall cease worrying about Lea.
Stupid to do so, in any case; but A.C. does not
speak lightly, and he said he was unhappy about
Lea's health, and that she had "given her life to
the Work".

Sept.15 When working fx on subconscious nervous system, I
seem to look out from the particular spot in which
I am working. Say, the lower leg. Is consciousness focussed there for the moment, or do mind &
leg so synchronize that it seems so? If so, why
not achieve Unity with this as a working basis?

p.m.   Took a long walk this afternoon. Reached a
state to-day where it seemed for a moment insanity would be a relief. Could I have broken myself
I should have done so.

Spet.16 And now I am thinking of the justification of some
of my acts!!

Sept.18 Letter from Lea! She is not well, but the uncertainty is over. (P.S. Did not realize three weeks
had elapsed since her last letter.)

Sept.19 500 lire from Fazio, as a loan.
Letter to Mary Pickford.

Sept.21 Resumed Pentagram - morning only to-day.

p.m.   Have been in a deplorable state - past two days especially I felt bruised and sore (in spirit?). This afternoon able to work internally, and help matters. What is this huge jelly-like substance? (Heretofore spoken of as 'mother of vinegar'. A dot of consciousness in this substance which seems to have odour, taste, or what? And does this dot of consciousness move from place to place, or no?

Sept.22   Took 2 sniffs of H.B. last night, and E. There is something for me to get out of this Shot-Drill. To the finite mind complete knowledge of the future, the pre-ordained, would mean insanity, annihilitation by fighting continually, stupefaction by drink or drugs, suicide, soddenness - depending on the mind obtaining such knowledge! The element of surprise, whether or joy or grief, pleasure or pain, keeps us interested in life. The hopelessness of the very poor makes them turn to drink or sexual excesses - they have no other relief.
The finite mind says, How horribly bored God must be!" If everything is known, how could it be otherwise?
Pentagram morning and evening henceforth.

Sept.25   I would like so much to get to a place where I could make money for this Abbey; the locality would make no difference. I enter this because one year ago, when the question of returning to the States came up, I found myself very reluctant. (I must state, however, I felt that move not to be my Will at the time.) Now I should be willing to drop any opportunities this place may afford for attainment, and could happily take myself where money could be commanded.

Spet.26   Started Pranayama to-day - an altogether different conception from anything heretofore acquired. Am away from breath control, body control, and into a finer matter. Something new to work for, and I feel invigorated.
My August experience left me in the plane of psychic (?) sensation. Discovered after a time that I smoked a cigarette to acquire this sensation, breathed to acquire it, etc. This entry should have been made a week ago, at the least, as I had rid myself fully of the desire by that time.

Sept.28 Letter to Mary K. re money.

Sept.29 Letter from Lea. No.3q.342. Just for a moment it
flashed across me that somewhere in the Ceremony,
or the getting of the Word, there had been a hitch
- which sounds perfectly ridiculous.

Oct. 2 Lea returned from London. Looking better than I
expected. Funny, she said the same thing about me.

Oct. 3 Lea looking fine. To see her no one would suspect
an illness of nervous breakdown. To-night I tried
her reflexes - left leg responded though not vig-
orously. Right knee gave a slight response.

Oct. 4 Lea has changed considerably. She is noticeably
freer of the personal. I assume this is a perma-
nent change, though her illness (Dr.Maggo says:
"Tuberculosis" and shakes his head) may explain a
part of it; she lacks her former 'pep'.
         I have now finished two coats, one for Howie
and one for Hansi, made out of two coats of the
Beast dug out of a trunk.

Oct. 8 Last night, in sleep, removed an oblong pillow
standing against the back of a couch, and discovered a hen (I think) standing on one leg. The
other leg - the right one - removed at the first
joint, was lying beside her.

Oct. 19 Think I have made a discovery which not only af-
fects me, but the majority of women. A.C. says
I have 'drivelled' about him. Maybe I have; which
is stupid. Most women look to a certain man, or
two, for deliverance - they know not from what.
I have been given to understand that A.C. is to be
my initiator - therefore I have thought of him,
looked to him. But, love? What is love? Now that
I look at the matter from this angle, do I really
love or am I merely anxious for the initiation
that I may understand and go on to my work? I assume the large majority of women whose life is
bound up in the men they have married are no more
in love than are the men - they simply have learned
a bit of self-expression, and needing this they
call it 'love'. Certainly I have known other men
who at the time attracted me more than A.C. has
ever done; though not being occultists the attraction would doubtless have worn off in time. (Ev-
en so, it would wear off eventually in any case;-
I cannot picture myself 'loving' one man all my
life.)

Oct. 20 I have not written lately: I feel that this record
         is closed, that when I start another I shall have
         begun a different phase of my career.

Oct. 25 1,000 lire transmitted by or through Pachou West
         of Los Angeles. (Mary K.)

         Beast returned from London Nov.4 - possibly two
         weeks later now.
         Continuing my entry of Oct.19.
         I have accepted what I understood to be my Destiny
         because I wanted to believe; I came to Cefalu be-
         cause of what was received by me automatically &
         during the initiation of May, 1918 - all in Cali-
         fornia. A.C.'s letter did not influence my com-
         ing beyond an inner conviction that what he there-
         in suggested was the correct interpretation of my
         message.
         I think I have now cleared my decks. All this is
         put aside - it has always lain at the back of my
         mind, whatever the conscious may have been doing.
         Now I stand free of all California influence, and
         of A.C. to the extent that I connected this man
         with the man I learned of while in California.
         Now I stand free.

Nov. 23 Am willing now to undertake an abhorred task - I
         must understand the why and wherefore; the where-
         from. So appallingly loathesome when first con-
         fronted - still so to the physical.

Dec. 22 In low state physically, mentally, spiritually for
some time. Last night in deep dejection I asked for light
         or help. Got the following:
         In a building which covered acres - in fact, knew
         of nothing but building, rooms, halls, galleries,
         etc. Two stories. A man "The Catch of the Season",
         was surrounded by a bevy of young women, the clever
         kind who are always at the centre of the chief int-
         erest. This group was continually on the move,
         upstairs and down. Once in passing the Man stopp-
         ed and said to me (I standing apart from any group
         but somehow linked with a less showy element): "If
         you .   .   .   .   I shall send you back."
         I replied: "I care nothing about those women."
         There was something about bathing. Found this
         impossible because the floor surrounding each tub
         - an oblong flush with the floor - gave way under
         my feet. A short matronly woman finally arranged
         a bath for me in a room where floor was solid.

Then I found myself downstairs at the dining table
of the Man's aunt, a tall, slender, aristocratic,
elegant woman of about 55. Rooms & halls here
sumptuous - many people.
The hour for tea was at hand, but no tea appeared.
I rose from the table, moved along a wide long
hall to right of reception rooms; curved to left &
found servants quarters. Lackeys (men in uniform)
came running from various doors bearing many dishes. I was surprised at the extent of the "Tea",
profuse and elaborate. The dishes were placed on
a large tea wagon. I accidentally spoilt the ap-

at my ap-
pearance

pearance of one dish by the edge of another; the
lackey much perturbed; I said, "Never mind, I will
tell the butler 'twas my fault", which I did then
& there, he just then showing up. (I in grey sat-
in of pinkish-lavendar tone, with veil floating
round my figure but not over my head.)
    I then found myself in a gallery to left of re-
ception rooms, and running parallel with them, the
people I saw there making a palaver and simpering
at me because I "sat at the Aunt's table!"
    Then I was walking along a garden path with the
Aunt, the garden otherwise empty. She informed me
she had chosen me for the mate of the Man. I
amazed - "Why me!" "Because in all the throng you
are the only one that thought of my tea." We came
to a tall building, decidedly phallic, the work-
shop of the nephew. Pagoda-like. We entered door
at side of the top. The Aunt said, "I will go down
first and make it easier for you." She suddenly
disappeared - impressed me as having fallen. I
peered anxiously over the edge, and found rising
up through centre of building, one-third of its
distance, a pillar of cement (round or square?);
rising out of this a number of pipes of different
lengths, iron, like gas or water pipes, out of
which steam was escaping. The Aunt rested her
body across some pipes, her head immediately below our entrance, her feet opposite. I got down
(how?) and placed my body at right angles, my feet
on pipes, my head or shoulders on her solar plexus.
    Next found myself at base of pillar, lying -
curled somewhat - face downward in utter abasement.
Woe filled me, and a feeling of intense shame. Simultaneously I head the Man's quick, firm step approaching; he was eager, triumphant. As he stood
by me I had a feeling he preferred another, though
I knew not whom. He stooped, my clothes came off
in his grasp. I lay, naked, my body whiteness it-

self. He was utterly content, and his vibration
one of the satisfaction of a dynamo at full speed
(I do not know how else to describe it; there was
nothing of the so-called 'human' about it). I en-
abled the dynamo to operate.

I then found myself on a ship's deck, seated
above and apart from the people on board, who moved
about as though in awe of me, spoke in whispers,
etc. I still the embodiment of woe. Finally a man,
feeling compassionate, stepped forward softly & re-
~~spectfully~~ reverentially, and said "He has gone to
arrange your passage; you are both sailing on the
........." (What was the name?) I realized then
that the Man was in the cabin of the Captain; that
the ship was not an ordinary one, it was quite dis-
tinctive, and was as the Ruler of all other vessels,
powerful and ~~most~~ swift.

I came out of this dream with the woe still upon me, though it passed off quickly.

In the afternoon Beast came in to wish me a Happy New Year. The sorrow rose again, I felt like
weeping up my boot-heels, and went out for a soli-
tary walk. But it availed me naught. Physically
too tired to go far.

Even.   A Solstice ceremony in Circle; very good indeed.
After retiring I realized that in order fully to
complete herself Woman had to achieve something in
which Man has no part. I.e. Woman may give up her
entire life to helping Man achieve his Will; it is
not sufficient for her.

I have a message for Woman ("You thought of my Tea",
i.e. Woman's affairs). Now to dig it out. Mine
the Cup and the Disk, Beast the Wand & Sword; thus
completing the whole. *claim the Cup and the Disk.* 1956, Nov.

*Did not fulfil
myself. So cannot*

Dec. 28 The load I have been carrying these two or three
weeks (the last few days not so heavily) has dropped from me, and I feel that the telling Lea of the
foregoing dream and our subsequent conversation af-
firmed my Will by a material act of Will; and that
this has eased me. I wonder is it so? It was not
altogether easy to say the Man in the dream was
Beast, but having gone that far I plunged still
farther. I told her I went to Cairo for my Initiation, and when she said: "I wonder if you are mentioned in the Book of the Law?", I answered "Many
times." But showed weakness by adding, "Time, of

No! Nothing of the sort.

course, will have to prove that." But by this willed action I entered the arena. To date my entire Cefalu career has been "Love under will". I now realize that my taking my proper chair at the Table must be an act of will. I must claim it; demand it, if so it be; knock down and walk over the supine body of any who might oppose my presence - should there be any such. To-day I sounded my first bugle. Also I can now understand Beast's declaring himself the O.H.O.

Temple of the Silver Star - Academic Track

The Temple of the Silver Star is a non-profit religious and educational corporation, based on the principles of Thelema. It was founded in service to the A∴A∴, under warrant from Soror Meral (Phyllis Seckler), to provide preparatory training in magick, mysticism, Qabalah, Tarot, astrology, and much more. In its academic track, each student is assigned an individual teacher, who provides one-to-one instruction and group classes. Online classes and other distance-learning options are available.

The criteria for admission to the academic track of the Temple are explained on the application itself, which may be submitted online via the T.O.T.S.S. website. The Temple has campuses or study groups in Sacramento, Oakland, Los Angeles, Reno, Seattle, Denver, Boston, West Chester (Philadelphia-area), Toronto, Japan, Austria and the U.K. Public classes are offered regularly; schedules are available on our website.

Temple of the Silver Star - Initiatory Track

The Temple of the Silver Star's initiatory track offers ceremonial initiation, personalized instruction, and a complete system of training in the Thelemic Mysteries. Our degree system is based on the Qabalistic Tree of Life and the cipher formulæ of the Golden Dawn, of which we are a lineal descendant.

Our entire curriculum is constructed to be in conformity with the Law of Thelema, and our central aim is to guide each aspirant toward the realization of their purpose in life, or True Will. In order to empower our members to discover and carry out their True Will, we teach Qabalah, Tarot, ceremonial magick, meditation, astrology, and much more. Our initiates meet privately for group ceremonial and healing work, classes, and other instruction. We occasionally offer public classes and rituals.

Active participation in a local Temple or Pronaos is the best way to maximize the benefits of our system. However, we do offer At-Large memberships for those living at some distance from one of our local bodies. If you are interested in learning more about our work, we invite you to download an application from our website and submit it to your nearest local body, or to contact us with any questions.

totss.org

Do what thou wilt shall be the whole of the Law.

The A∴A∴ is the system of spiritual attainment established by Aleister Crowley and George Cecil Jones in the early 1900s, as a modern expression of the Inner School of wisdom that has existed for millennia. Its central aim is simply to lead each aspirant toward their own individual attainment, for the betterment of all humanity. The course of study includes a diversity of training methods, such as Qabalah, raja yoga, ceremonial magick, and many other traditions.

A∴A∴ is not organized into outer social organizations, fraternities or schools; rather, it is based on the time-tested power of individual teacher-student relationships, under the guidance of the masters of the Inner School. All training and testing is done strictly in accordance with *Liber 185* and other foundational documents. Those interested in pursuing admission into A∴A∴ are invited to initiate contact via the following addresses:

A∴A∴

PO Box 215483

Sacramento, CA 95821

Onestarinsight.org

The Student phase of preparation for work in A∴A∴ begins by acquiring a specific set of reference texts, notifying A∴A∴ of the same, and studying the texts for at least three months. The Student may then request Examination. More information about this process is available via the Cancellarius at the addresses given above. Please use only these contact addresses when initiating correspondence. NOTE: While our primary contact address is in California, supervising Neophytes are available in many countries around the world.

If you are called to begin this journey, we earnestly invite you to contact us. Regardless of your choice in this matter, we wish you the best as you pursue your own Great Work. May you attain your True Will!

Love is the law, love under will.